THE WORLD'S GREATEST AIRCRAFT
MILITARY AIRCRAFT

THE WORLD'S GREATEST AIRCRAFT
MILITARY AIRCRAFT

Christopher Chant: edited by Michael J.H. Taylor

Chelsea House Publishers • Philadelphia

Published in 2000 by
Chelsea House Publishers
1974 Sproul Road, Suite 400
P.O. Box 914
Broomall. PA, 19008-0914

ISBN 0-7910-5420-9

Photographs on pages 2, 3, 4, 5, 6–7, 8, 27, 28, 40 courtesy
Michael J.H. Taylor

Printed in China

Library of Congress Cataloging-in-Publication Data

Chant Christopher.
    Military aircraft / by Christopher Chant.
        p.   cm. -- (The world's greatest aircraft)
Originally published as part of the author's: The world's
greatest aircraft. London: Grange Books, 1997.
    Includes index.
    Summary: Drawings, photographs, and text describe a
variety of military aircraft, both U.S. and foreign, including
the Martin Marauder, Tupolev Badger, Dassault Mirage,
Handley Page Victor, and Grumman Hawkeye.
    ISBN 0-7910-5420-9 (hc.)
    1. Airplanes, Military Juvenile literature. [1. Airplanes,
Military.] I. Title. II. Series.
UG1240.C483 1999
623.7'46--do21
                                                99-30416
                                                CIP

Page 2: Tornado GR4 – development aircraft
Page 3: Dassault Mirage 1V-P refuelling
Right: Sea Harrier F/A2
Frontispiece: F-14D

Light/Medium Bombers

The light bomber is arguably the oldest recorded form of combat aircraft. The first known illustration of an aerial attacker dates from 1326, as a bomb-carrying pennon kite, and thereby easily predates depictions in art of bomb-carrying balloons. Interestingly, more than a decade before the American Wright brothers achieved the world's first recognized manned and powered aeroplane flight, the first-ever contract to build a military heavier-than-air aeroplane had been issued to France's famed pioneer, Clément Ader, in 1892. Ader's aeroplane was to be a two-seater capable of carrying 75 kg (165 lb) of bombs; but the machine proved unable to fly during trials in 1897 and so the contract was not completed.

In one of the first demonstrations of how aeroplanes could be used offensively in war, in January 1910 American Lt. Paul Beck dropped sandbags over Los Angeles from an aeroplane piloted by Louis Paulhan. More significantly, American pioneer Glenn Curtiss dropped dummy bombs over Lake Keuka in June that year, using buoys to indicate the outline of a battleship to be attacked from low level. Then, in January 1911, Lt. Myron Crissy and Philip Parmalee released explosive bombs from their Wright biplane during live trials over San Francisco.

Italy was the first to take aeroplanes to war, in 1911, and that November Second Lt. Giulio Gavotti piloted an aeroplane from which Cipelli grenades were thrown by hand onto Turkish forces at Taguira Oasis and Ain Zara (Libya), the first-ever recorded bombing raid by aeroplane. Fighting in Mexico provided the backdrop for the first aeroplane bombing of a warship when Didier Masson, supporting the forces of General Alvarado Obregon, attacked Mexican gunships in Guaymas Bay. During this conflict, Mexican generals often used the services of foreign pilots, and it is curious to note that in Mexico in November 1913 the very first aerial combat took place between aircraft, yet neither pilot exchanged pistol fire was Mexican!

With the outbreak of World War I, tiny aircraft immediately undertook both nuisance and strategic bombing raids on the enemy, but in essence were the lightest of bombers. From a tactical standpoint, the first missions of real significance came on May 1915, when British aircraft attacked the railway system bringing up German reinforcements during the Neuve Chapelle offensive, thereby working in direct support of British ground forces. Areas around Courtrai and Menin were raided, plus the stations at Don, Douai and Lille, while for good measure three other aircraft bombed the German Divisional Headquarters at Fournes. The light bomber had established its importance as a tactical weapon and, despite the appearance of the much larger bombing aeroplanes possessing greater range and warload, the light bomber in developed forms remained an essential part of air forces from this time forward.

Post World War I, the medium bomber bridged the gap between light and heavy types, although the definition became blurred as some air forces used payload carried as the defining factor, while others used range. Some difficulty in pinning down an exact definition continued until after World War II, when new light bomber jets such as the RAF's Canberra that could carry a nuclear weapon to the U.S.S.R. caused further erosion of reasonable definitions.

Today, only a few air forces field heavy bombers, and it is probably true to say that the only truly modern medium bomber currently operational is the Russian Tu-22M *Backfire*, although even this is more often referred to as an intermediate-range bomber. Instead, many forces rely on smaller high-speed or subsonic jet attack aircraft armed with free-fall or precision-guided weapons. These, after all, can often carry a bomb load in excess of those managed by heavy bombers during World War II. 'Interdiction', 'strike', 'ground attack' and 'close air support' are all modern-day terms for the varied traditional roles of the smaller bomber, and many (such as Tornado, Mirage 2000N and Sukhoi Su-24/Su-34) could, if called upon, carry out strategic as well as tactical attacks if the target was not too distant. Smaller jets have often been used at the outset of regional conflicts to deliver crippling blows against enemy forces, their size better suiting pinpoint attacks against high-value or critical targets. Indeed, air power in all forms has proven to be decisive in modern campaigns.

Picture: Italy and Brazil collaborated on development of the AMX International AMX close air support and interdiction jet, entering service from 1989 and capable of delivering 3,800 kg (8,378 lb) of free-fall and guided weapons

BREGUET 14 (France)

Bre.14B2

The Breguet Bre. 14 was France's single most important and successful warplane of World War I, and perhaps the best known French combat plane until the advent of the Dassault Mirage III series. The type began to take shape on the drawing boards of the company's designers during the summer of 1916, and the first AV Type XIV flew in November 1916 with the AV (Avant, or forward) signifying that the plane was of the tractor type. Though not notable for its aesthetic qualities, the machine that soon became the Type 14 and later

the Bre. 14 was immensely sturdy as a result of its steel, duralumin and wooden construction covered in fabric and light alloy panels and supported on strong landing gear of the spreader type. The pilot and gunner were located close together in the optimum tactical location, and the front

mounted Renault in line engine proved both powerful and reliable.

An initial 150 aircraft were ordered in the A.2 two-seat artillery observation category during April 1917, and by the end of that year orders had been placed for 2,650 aircraft to be produced by Breguet and five licensees in two-seat A.2 artillery and B.2 bomber variants, the latter with wings of increased span and flaps on the trailing edges of the lower wing. Other World War I variants were the Bre. 14B.1 single-seat bomber and Bre. 14S ambulance. Production up to the end of World War I totalled 5,300 aircraft with a variety of engine types, and more than 2,500 additional aircraft were built before production ended in 1928. Many of the post-war aircraft were of the Bre. 14 TOE type for use in France's colonial possessions. The Bre. 14 was finally phased out of French service only in 1932. Substantial exports were also made.

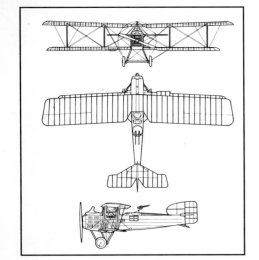

Breguet Bre.14

BREGUET Bre.14B2
Role: Fast day bomber/reconnaissance
Crew/Accommodation: Two
Power Plant: One 300 hp Renault 12 Fcy water-cooled inline
Dimensions: Span 14.91 m (48.92 ft); length 8.87 m (29.10 ft); wing area 51.1 m² (550 sq ft)
Weights: Empty 1,035 kg (2,282 lb); MTOW 1,580 kg (3,483 lb)
Performance: Maximum speed 195 km/h (121 mph) at sea level; operational ceiling 4,265 m (13,993 ft); range 485 km (301 miles) with full warload
Load: Two/three .303 inch machine guns, plus up to 260 kg (573 lb) of externally-carried bombs

A Breguet Bre.14 in Portuguese service

AIRCO (de HAVILLAND) D.H.9 and D.H.9A (United Kingdom)

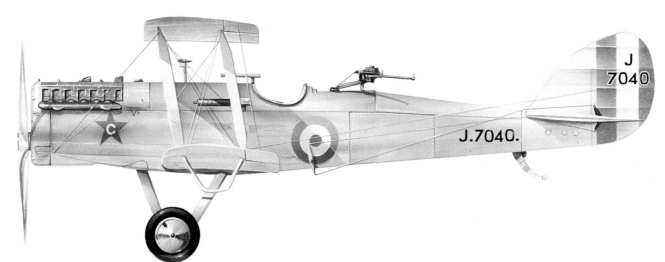

D.H.9A

The D.H.9 was planned as a longer-range successor to the D.H.4. To speed production, the D.H.4's flying surfaces and landing gear were combined with a new fuselage that located the pilot and gunner close together and provided better streamlining for the engine, in this instance a 171.5-kW (230-hp) Galloway-built BHP engine. The type first flew in July 1917, and proved so successful that outstanding D.H.4 contracts were converted to the D.H.9, which therefore entered large-scale production with the 224-kW (300-hp) lightweight version of the BHP developed by Siddeley-Deasy and known as the Puma. The engine was unreliable and generally derated to 171.5 kW (230 hp), which gave the D.H.9 performance inferior to that of the D.H.4. As a result, the D.H.9 suffered quite heavy losses when it entered service during April 1918 over the Western Front, though it fared better in poorer defended areas, such as Macedonia and Palestine. Some 3,200 D.H.9s were built by Airco and 12 subcontractors.

Given the fact that the D.H.9's failing was its engine, it was hoped that use of the excellent 280-kW (375-hp) Rolls-Royce Eagle VIII would remedy the situation, but demands on this motor were so great that an American engine, the 298-kW (400-hp) Packard Liberty 12, was used instead to create the D.H.9A, which was perhaps the best strategic bomber of World War I. British production of 885 aircraft was complemented by 1,415 American-built Engineering Division USD-9 aircraft.

AIRCO D.H.9
Role: Light day bomber
Crew/Accommodation: Two
Power Plant: One 230 hp Siddeley-Deasy B.H.P. water-cooled inline
Dimensions: Span 12.92 m (42.4 ft); length 9.28 m (30.46 ft); wing area 40.32 m² (430 sq ft)
Weights: Empty 1,012 kg (2,230 lb); MTOW 1,508 kg (3,325 lb)
Performance: Maximum speed 177 km/h (110 mph) at 3,048 m (10,000 ft); operational ceiling 4.724 m (15,500 ft); endurance 4.5 hours
Load: Two .303 inch machine guns, plus up to 412 kg (908 lb) bombload

Airco D.H.9A

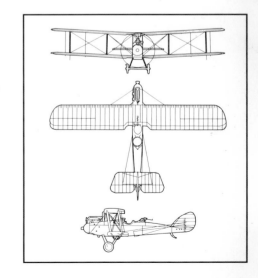

Airco (de Havilland) D.H.9

BREGUET 19 (France)

Breguet 19

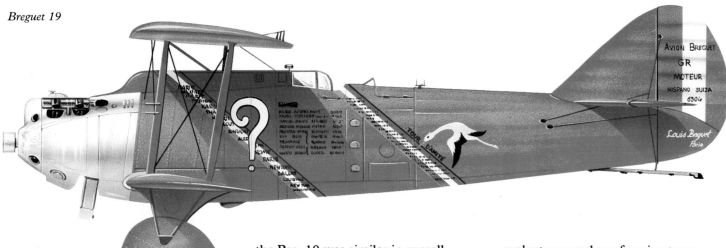

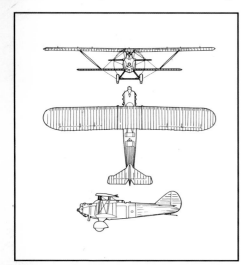

Breguet 19

First flown in March 1922 with a 336-kW (450-hp) Renault 12Kb inline engine, the Bre. 19 was planned as successor to the Bre. 14 but was produced in parallel with its predecessor for service with units based in metropolitan France. Though

the Bre. 19 was similar in overall concept to the Bre. 14, it was a considerably more pleasing and aerodynamically refined design with unequal- rather than almost-equal span wings with single outward sloping I-type interplane struts, a circular-section rather than slab-sided fuselage, and a much cleaner landing gear arrangement with a spreader-type main unit. The structure was primarily of duralumin with fabric covering, though the forward fuselage as far aft as the gunner's cockpit was covered with duralumin sheet.

The prototype was followed by 11 development aircraft that were used to

evaluate a number of engine types, and the Bre. 19 entered production in 1923. By 1927 some 2,000 aircraft had been delivered, half each in the

B.2 bomber and A.2 spotter/reconnaissance roles. Most aircraft in French service were powered by the Renault 12K or Lorraine-Dietrich 12D/E engines, and with each type gave invaluable service mainly at home but also in France's colonial wars of the 1920s in Morocco and Syria. The Bre. 19 soldiered on into obsolescence, and late in its career equipped four night fighter squadrons before being relegated to the reserve and training roles during 1934. The type also secured considerable export success (direct sales and licensed production) mainly of the Bre. 19GR long-range variant. The Bre. 19 was also developed in Bidon (petrol can) and Super Bidon variants for a number of classic record-breaking distance flights.

BREGUET Bre. 19 B2
Role: Light day bomber
Crew/Accommodation: Two
Power Plant: One 550 hp Renault 12Kc water-cooled inline
Dimensions: Span 14.8 m (48.5 ft); length 8.89 m (29.16 ft); wing area 50 m² (538.4 sq ft)
Weights: Empty 1,485 kg (3,273 lb); MTOW 2,301 kg (5,093 lb)
Performance: Maximum speed 240 km/h (149 mph) at sea level; operational ceiling 7,800 m (25,590 ft); range 800 km (497 miles) with full warload
Load: Three/four .303 inch machine guns, plus up to 700 kg (1,543 lb) of bombs

Breguet 19TR

JUNKERS Ju 87 (Germany)

Ju 87B-1

A pair of Ju 87B aircraft

The Ju 87 was planned as a dedicated dive-bomber, a type known to the Germans as the *Sturzkampfflugzeug* or Stuka, and proved a decisive weapon in the opening campaigns of World War II. The type delivered its weapons with great accuracy, and came to be feared so highly that the appearance of its inverted gull wings and the sound of the 'Jericho trumpet' sirens on its landing gear legs often caused panic.

The first of four prototypes flew late in 1935 as the Ju 87 V1 with the 477-kW (640-hp) Rolls-Royce Kestrel V inline engine and endplate vertical surfaces. The next two prototypes had single vertical tail surfaces and were powered by the 455-kW (610-hp) Junkers Jumo 210Aa inline, while the last prototype introduced a larger

vertical tail. The type entered service in the spring of 1937 as the Ju 87A with the 477-kW (640-hp) Jumo 210C, and production of this variant totalled 210 aircraft.

Later variants included the Ju 87B with the 895-kW (1,200-hp) Jumo 211D, a larger canopy, and the wheel fairings replaced by spats, the Ju 87D dive-bomber and ground-attack type with the 1051-kW (1,410-hp) Jumo 211J, in a revised cowling, a redesigned canopy, a still larger vertical tail, simplified landing gear, and upgraded offensive and defensive features, the Ju 87G anti-tank model with two 37-mm underwing cannon, the Ju 87H conversion of the Ju 87D as a dual-control trainer, and the Ju 87R version of the Ju 87B in the long-range anti-ship role. From 1941 the Ju 87's limitations in the face of effective anti-aircraft and fighter defences were fully evident, but Germany lacked a replacement and the type had to remain in service as increasingly specialized ground-attack and anti-tank aircraft. Production of the series totalled 5,709 aircraft.

JUNKERS Ju 87B
Role: Dive bomber
Crew/Accommodation: Two
Power Plant: One 1,200 hp Junkers Jumo 211 Da water-cooled inline
Dimensions: Span 13.8 m (45.3 ft); length 11 m (36.83 ft); wing are a 31.9 m² (343.3 sq ft)
Weights: Empty 2,750 kg (6,063 lb); MTOW 4,250 kg (9,321 lb)
Performance: Maximum speed 380 km/h (237 mph) at 4,000 m (13,124 ft); operational ceiling 8,100 m (26,575 ft); range 600 km (372 miles) with full warload
Load: Three 7.9 mm machine guns, plus 1,000 kg (2,205 lb) bombload

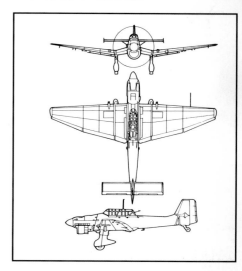

Junkers Ju 87B-2

13

HEINKEL He 111 (Germany)

He 111H-5

The He 111 was Germany's most important bomber of World War II, and was built to the extent of 7,300 or more aircraft. The type was designed supposedly as an airliner, and in its first form it was basically an enlarged He 70 with two 492-kW (660-hp) BMW VI 6,0Z inline engines mounted on the wings. The first prototype flew in February 1935, and considerable development was necessary in another prototype, 10 pre-production aircraft and finally another prototype before the He 111B began to enter military

service with 746-kW (1,000-hp) Daimler-Benz DB 600 inlines, which were also used for the six He 111C 10-passenger airliners. The DB 600 was in short supply, so the He 111E used the 746-kW (1,000-hp) Junkers Jumo 211A and was developed in five subvariants to a total of about 190 aircraft.

The 70 He 111Fs combined the wing of the He 111G with Jumo 211A-3 engines, and at the same time the eight He 111Gs introduced a wing of straight rather than curved taper and was built in variants with BMW 132 radial or DB 600 inline engines. The He 111H was based on the He 111P and became the most

extensively built model, some 6,150 aircraft being produced in many important subvariants, both built and converted, up to the He 111H-23 with increasingly powerful engines (including the Jumo 211 and 213), heavier armament and sophisticated equipment. The He 111J was a torpedo bomber, and about 90 were delivered. Despite its late designation, the He 111P was

introduced in 1939 and pioneered the asymmetric and extensively glazed forward fuselage in place of the original stepped design, and about 40 aircraft were built in subvariants up to the He 111P-6.

The oddest variant was the He 111Z heavy glider tug, which was two He 111H-6 bombers joined by a revised wing section incorporating a fifth Jumo 211F engine.

HEINKEL HE 111H-16
Role: Bomber
Crew/Accommodation: Five
Power Plant: Two 1,350 hp Junkers Jumo 211F-2 water-cooled inlines
Dimensions: Span 22.6 m (74.15 ft); length 16.4 m (53.81 ft); wing area 86.5 m² (931 sq ft)
Weights: Empty 8,680 kg (19,136 lb); MTOW 14,000 kg (30,865 lb)
Performance: Maximum speed 435 km/h (270 mph) at 6,000 m (19,685 ft); operational ceiling 6,700 m (21,982 ft); range 1,950 km (1,212 miles) with maximum bombload
Load: Two 20 mm cannon and five 13 mm machine guns, plus up to 3,600 kg (7,937 lb) of bombs

Heinkel He 111D-1

Heinkel He 111H bombers

DORNIER Do 17 Family (Germany)

Do 217K

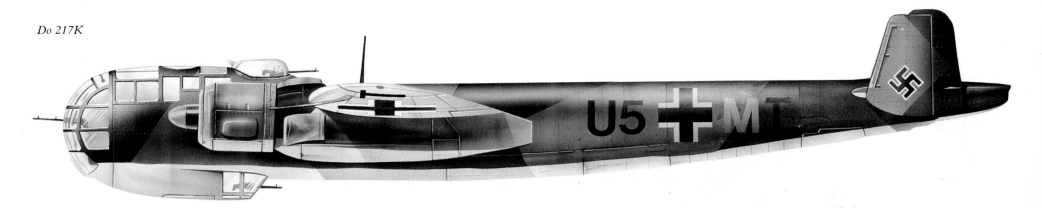

The origins of this important German bomber lie with a 1933 Deutsche Lufthansa requirement for a six-passenger mailplane, though this requirement was also responsible for the narrow 'pencil' fuselage that was one of the main hindrances to the type's later development as a warplane. The Do 17 first flew in the autumn of 1934, and its performance suggested a military development with the single vertical tail surface replaced by endplate surfaces to increase the dorsal gunner's field of fire. Six military prototypes were followed by two pre-production types, the Do 17E-1 bomber with a shortened but glazed nose and 500-kg (1,102-lb) bomb load, and the Do 17F-1 photographic reconnaissance type, both powered by 559-kW (750-hp) BMW VI inlines.

There followed a number of experimental and limited-production variants before the advent of the Do 17Z definitive bomber built in several subvariants with the 746-kW (1,000-hp) BMW-Bramo 323 Fafnir radials in 1939 and 1940. Do 17 production was perhaps 1,200 aircraft, and from this basic type was developed the Do 215, of which 112 were produced with Daimler-Benz DB 601A inline engines. The two main models were the Do 215B-4 reconnaissance type and the Do 215B-5 night fighter. The Do 217 that first flew in September 1938 was essentially a Do 17 with 802-kW (1,075-hp) DB 601A engines, a larger fuselage, and a revised empennage.

Production was 1,750 aircraft in three basic series: the Do 217E heavy bomber and anti-ship type with stepped forward fuselage and 1178-kW (1,580-hp) BMW 801 radial engines, the Do 217K and Do 217M heavy night bomber and missile-armed anti-ship types with unstepped forward fuselage plus 1268-kW (1,700-hp) BMW 801 radials and 1305-kW (1,750-hp) DB 603A inline engines, and the Do 217N night fighter and intruder types with radar, specialist weapon fit, and 1379-kW (1,850-hp) DB 603A inline engines.

The Do 217P, the final development of the Dornier Do 217 series

DORNIER Do 17Z-2
Role: Medium bomber
Crew/Accommodation: Five
Power Plant: Two 1,000 hp BMW Bramo 323P Fafnir air-cooled radials
Dimensions: Span 18 m (59.06 ft); length 15.8 m (51.84 ft); wing area 55 m² (592 sq ft)
Weights: Empty 5,210 kg (11,488 lb); MTOW 8,590 kg (18,940 lb)
Performance: Maximum speed 410 km/h (255 mph) at 4,000 m (13,124 ft); operational ceiling 8,200 m (26,904 ft); radius 330 km (205 miles) with full bombload
Load: Eight 7.9 mm machine guns, plus up to 1,000 kg (2,205 lb) of bombs

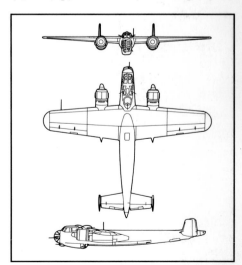

Dornier Do 217E-2

BRISTOL BLENHEIM (United Kingdom)

Blenheim Mk IF

L6798

NG⊙ L6798

In 1934 Lord Rothermere commissioned Bristol to produce a fast and capacious light personal transport. This appeared as the Type 142 that first flew in April 1935 with two 485-kW (650-hp) Bristol Mercury VIS radials. The aircraft caused a

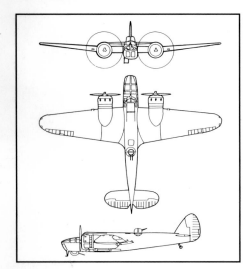

Bristol Blenheim Mk IV

great stir as it was 48 km/h (30 mph) faster than the U.K.'s latest fighter, and it was presented to the nation by the air-minded Rothermere after the Air Ministry asked for permission to evaluate the machine as a light bomber. As a result, Bristol developed the Type 142M bomber prototype that first flew in June 1936. The type offered higher performance than current light bombers, and was ordered in large numbers for service from 1937 onwards.

BRISTOL BLENHEIM Mk I
Role: Medium bomber
Crew/Accommodation: Three
Power Plant: Two 840 hp Bristol Mercury VIII air-cooled radials
Dimensions: Span 17.17 m (56.33 ft); length 12.11 m (39.75 ft); wing area 43.57 m² (469 sq ft)
Weights: Empty 3,674 kg (8,100 lb); MTOW 5,670 kg (12,500 lb)
Performance: Maximum speed 459 km/h (285 mph) at 4,572 m (15,000 ft); operational ceiling 8,315 m (27,280 ft); range 1,810 km (1,125 miles) with full bombload
Load: Two .303 inch machine guns, plus up to 454 kg (1,000 lb) of bombs

The main variants were the original Blenheim Mk I of which 1,365 were built in the U.K. and 61 under licence (45 in Finland and 16 in Yugoslavia) with 626-kW (840-hp) Mercury VIII radials, the Blenheim Mk IF interim night fighter of which about 200 were produced as conversions with radar and a ventral pack of four machine guns, the generally improved Blenheim Mk IV of which 3,297 were built in the U.K. and another 10 under licence in Finland with 686-kW (920-hp) Mercury XV engines, more fuel and a lengthened nose, the Blenheim Mk IVF extemporized night fighter, the Blenheim Mk IVF fighter conversion, and the Blenheim Mk V of which 945 were built with 708-kW (950-hp) Mercury 25 or 30 engines and a solid nose housing four machine-guns in Mk VA bomber, Mk VB close support, Mk VC operational trainer and Mk VD tropicalized bomber subvariants. The Blenheim Mk IV was built in Canada as the Bolingbroke coastal reconnaissance

and light bomber aircraft, of which 676 were built as Mk Is with Mercury VIIIs, Mk IVs with Mercury XVs and MK IV Ws with Pratt & Whitney R-1830 Wasp radials.

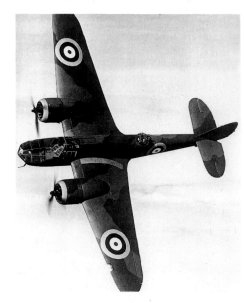

Bristol Blenheim Mk IV

SAVOIA-MARCHETTI SM. 79 SPARVIERO (Italy)

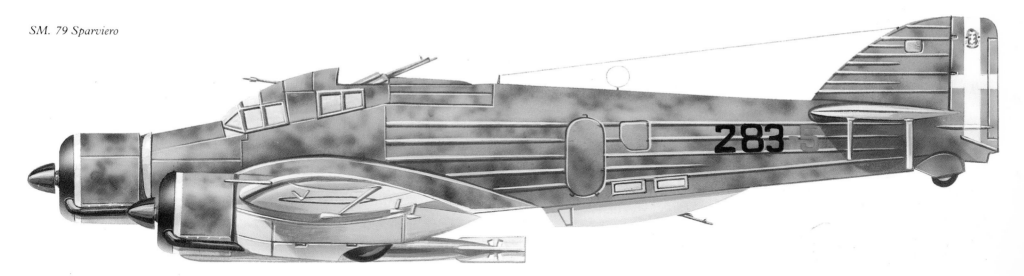

SM. 79 Sparviero

The SM. 79 Sparviero (Sparrowhawk) was Italy's most important bomber of World War II and, in its specialist anti-ship version, the best torpedo bomber of the war. The type was evolved from the company's earlier tri-motor types, and first flew in late 1934 as the SM. 79P prototype of a planned eight-passenger civil transport, and in this form was powered by three 455-kW (610-hp) Piaggio Stella radials. The type was a cantilever low-wing monoplane of mixed construction with retractable tailwheel landing gear, and its considerable capabilities soon

prompted the adoption of a more warlike role with a revised cockpit, a vental gondola, provision for offensive and defensive armament, and 582-kW (780-hp) Alfa Romeo 125 RC 35/126 RC 34 radial engines.

Production of the series totalled about 1,370 for Italy and for export, and the initial variant was the SM. 79-I bomber with 582-kW (780-hp) Alfa-Romeo 126 RC 34 radials and no windows in the fuselage sides. This type was successfully evaluated in the Spanish Civil War in both the level bomber and the torpedo bomber roles,

and proved so admirable in the latter that a specialized variant was then ordered as the SM. 79-II torpedo bomber with 746-kW (1,000-hp) Piaggio P.XI RC 40 or 768-kW (1,030-hp) Fiat A.80 RC 41 radials and provision for two 450-mm (17.7-in) torpedoes. The SM. 79-III was an improved version of the SM. 79-II without the ventral gondola and with heavier defensive armament. Production of the SM. 79-I, II and III totalled 1,230. Other variants were the SM. 79B twin-engined export version

of the SM. 79-I with a variety of radials, the SM.79C (and SM. 79T long-range) prestige conversion of the SM. 79-I without dorsal and ventral protusions, the SM.79JR model for Romania with two Junkers Jumo 211Da inline engines, the SM.79K version of the SM. 79-I for Yugoslavia, and the SM. 83 civil transport version.

Savoia-Marchetti SM. 79C

SAVOIA-MARCHETTI SM.79 SPARVIERO
Role: Bomber
Crew/Accommodation: Four
Power Plant: Three 780 hp Alfa Romeo 126 RC34 air-cooled radials
Dimensions: Span 21 m (69.55 ft); length 15.62 m (51.25 ft); wing area 61.7 m² (664.2 sq ft)
Weights: Empty 6,800 kg (14,991 lb); MTOW 10,500 kg (23,148 lb)
Performance: Maximum speed 430 km/h (267 mph) at 4,000 m (13,125 ft); operational ceiling 6,500 m (21,325 ft); range 1,900 km (1,180 miles) with full bombload
Load: Three 12.7 mm and two 7.7 mm machine guns, plus up to 1,250 kg (2,756 lb) of bombs or one torpedo

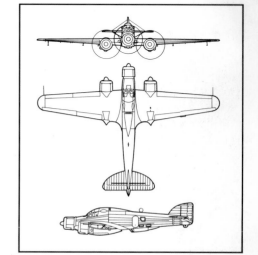

SM. 79-II Sparviero

JUNKERS Ju 88 Family (Germany)

Ju 88A-4

The Ju 88 can be considered Germany's equivalent to the British Mosquito and with that type was certainly the most versatile warplane of World War II. Production of the Ju 88 family totalled about 15,000 aircraft. The type was schemed as a high-speed bomber and first flew in December 1936 with 746-kW (1,000-hp) Daimler-Benz DB 600A inlines, subsequently changed to Junkers Jumo 211s of the same rating, a low/mid-set wing and, in the standard German fashion, the crew grouped closely together in an extensively glazed nose section that proved comparatively vulnerable despite steadily heavier defensive armament. With the Jumo 211, the Ju 88A entered widespread service, being built in variants up to the Ju 88A-17. Six manufacturers produced about 7,000 of this series alone.

The next operational bomber was the Ju 88S in three subvariants with the 1268-kW (1,700-hp) BMW 801G radial, smoother nose contours, and reduced bomb load to improve performance; companion reconnaissance models were the two variants of the Ju 88T and the three variants of the longer-range Ju 88H. Production of the Ju 88H/S/T series totalled some 550 aircraft. From the Ju 88A was developed the Ju 88C heavy fighter; this had BMW 801A radials and a 'solid' nose for the heavy gun armament, together with radar in a few night fighter variants. The definitive night fighter series with steadily improving radar and effective armament was the Ju 88G, together with the improved Ju 88R version of the Ju 88C. Other series were the Ju 88D long-range reconnaissance and Ju 88P anti-tank aircraft. Development of the same concept yielded the high-performance Ju 188 and high-altitude Ju 388 series.

Junkers Ju 88A-4 bombers

JUNKERS Ju 88A-4
Role: Light fast bomber
Crew/Accommodation: Four
Power Plant: Two 1,340 hp Junkers Jumo 211J-1 water-cooled inlines
Dimensions: Span 20 m (65.63 ft); length 14.4 m (47.23 ft); wing area 54.5 m² (586.6 sq ft)
Weights: Empty 9,860 kg (21,737 lb); MTOW 14,000 kg (30,870 lb)
Performance: Maximum speed 470 km/h (292 mph) at 5,300 m (17,390 ft); operational ceiling 8,200 m (26,900 ft); range, 1,790 km (1,112 miles) with full bombload
Load: Two 13 mm and three 7.9 mm machine guns, plus up to 2,000 kg (4,409 lb) bombload

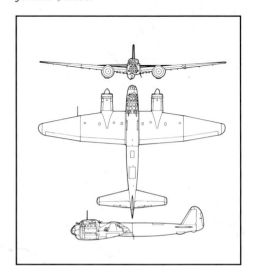

Junkers Ju 88A-4

VICKERS WELLINGTON (United Kingdom)

Wellington B.Mk III

The Wellington was the most important British medium bomber of World War II, and indeed during the early stages of the war was perhaps the only truly effective night bomber after the type was switched to this role in the aftermath of some disastrously heavy losses in early daylight raids. A Wellington of No. 149 Squadron was responsible for dropping the RAF's first 4,000-lb 'block buster' bomb during an attack on Emden in April 1941, and on the first RAF 'thousand bomber' raid on Germany (Cologne) in May 1942, no fewer than 599 of the 1,046 bombers used were Wellingtons.

Designed to meet a 1932 requirement, the prototype first flew in June 1936 with 682-kW (915-hp) Bristol Pegasus X radials. The type used the geodetic lattice-work form of airframe construction pioneered in the Vickers Wellesley by inventor Barnes Wallis, and was thus immensely strong. When production ceased in October 1945, no fewer than 11,461 Wellingtons had been produced in versions with the 746-kW (1,000-hp) Pegasus XVIII radial (the Wellington B.Mks I, IA and IC with steadily improved defensive capability, and the Wellington GR.Mk VIII with searchlight and provision for anti-submarine weapons), the 1,119-kW (1,500-hp) Bristol Hercules radial (the Wellington B.Mk III with the Hercules XI and B.Mk X with the Hercules VI or XVI, and the Wellington GR.Mks XI, XII, XIII and XIV with the Hercules VI or XVI and steadily improved anti-submarine equipment), the 783-kW (1,050-hp) Pratt & Whitney Twin Wasp radial (the Wellington B.Mk IV) and the 854-kW (1,145-hp) Rolls-Royce Merlin X inline (the Wellington B.Mks II and VI). Wellingtons were extensively converted later in the type's career into alternative roles such as freighting and training. Several aircraft were also used as engine test-beds, and the basic concept was developed considerably further in the Type 294 Warwick that was designed as a heavy bomber but actually matured as a maritime reconnaissance aircraft.

Vickers Wellington Mk III

VICKERS WELLINGTON B.Mk IC
Role: Heavy bomber
Crew/Accommodation: Five/six
Power Plant: Two 1,050 hp Bristol Pegasus XVIII air-cooled radials
Dimensions: Span 26.27 m (86.18 ft); length 19.69 m (64.6 ft); wing area 78 m² (848 sq ft)
Weights: Empty 8,709 kg (19,200 lb); MTOW 12,927 kg (28,500 lb)
Performance: Maximum speed 378 km/h (235 mph) at 1,440 m (4,724 ft); operational ceiling 5,486 m (18,000 ft); range 2,575 km (1,600 miles) with 925 kg (2,040 lb) bombload
Load: Six .303 inch machine guns, plus up to 2,041 kg (4,500 lb) internally stowed bombload

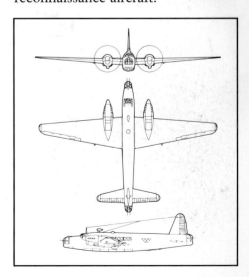

Vickers Wellington Mk II

AICHI D3A 'VAL' (Japan)

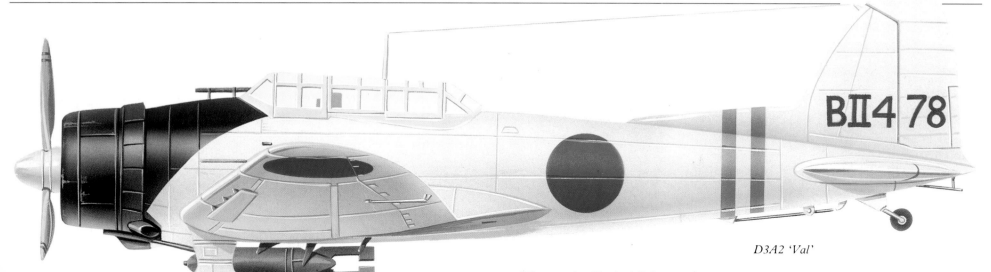

D3A2 'Val'

Designed as successor to the same company's D1A and first flown in 1938 with the 544-kW (730-hp) Kinsei 3 radial engine, the D3A was

Japan's most important naval dive-bomber at the beginning of World War II, and played a major part in the Pearl Harbor attack. Known to the Allies as the 'Val', the D3A played a decisive part in Japan's expansionist campaign in South-East Asia and the South-West Pacific, but was eclipsed by American carrierborne fighters from mid-1942 onward.

The type's elliptical flying surfaces were aerodynamically elegant, and the combination of a lightweight structure and fixed but spatted landing gear provided good performance. Production aircraft were based on the second prototype, but with slightly reduced span and also a long dorsal fin to improve directional stability. Total construction was 1,495 aircraft, and the main variants were the D3A1 and D3A2, which totalled 476 and 1,007 respectively.

The D3A1 entered service in 1940 with the 746-kW (1,000-hp) Kinsei 43

that was altered later in the production run to the 1,070-hp (798-kW) Kinsei 44 radial. The D3A2 was fitted with a propeller spinner and a modified rear cockpit canopy, and was powered by the 969-kW (1,300-hp) Kinsei 54 that could draw on greater fuel capacity for better performance and range. The D3A2-K was a trainer conversion of the earlier models. From late 1942 the type was relegated to the land-based attack role, and then to second-line tasks such as training before final use as kamikaze attack aircraft.

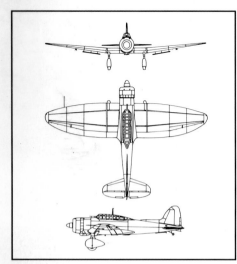

Aichi D3A2 'Val'

AICHI D3A2 'VAL'
Role: Naval carrierborne dive bomber
Crew/Accommodation: Two
Power Plant: One 1,300-hp Mitsubishi Kinsei 54 air-cooled radial
Dimensions: Span 14.37 m (47.1 ft); length 10.23 m (33.6 ft); wing area 23.6 m² (254 sq ft)
Weights: Empty 2,618 kg (5,722 lb); MTOW 4,122 kg (9,087 lb)
Performance: Maximum speed 430 km/h (267 mph) at 9,225 m (20,340 ft); operational ceiling 10,888 m (35,720 ft); range 1,561 km (970 miles)
Load: Three 7.7-mm machine guns, plus up to 370 kg (816 lb) of bombs

The Aichi D3A2

DOUGLAS SBD DAUNTLESS (U.S.A.)

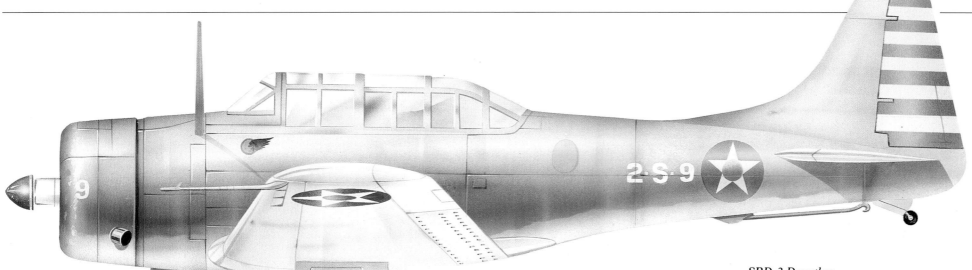

SBD-3 Dauntless

The SBD Dauntless was the most successful dive-bomber produced by the Americans during World War II, and assumed historical importance as one of the weapons that checked the tide of Japanese expansion in the Battles of the Coral Sea and Midway during 1942. The type began life as a development of the 1938 Northrop

BT-1 after Northrop's acquisition by Douglas. The Douglas development was first flown in July 1938 as the XBT-2 low-wing, monoplane with the 746-kW (1,000-hp) Wright R-1820-32 Cyclone radial engine, perforated split trailing-edge flaps that also served as airbrakes, and the main bomb carried under the fuselage on a crutch that swung it clear of the propeller before it was released in a steep dive.

The type began to enter U.S. Navy carrierborne and U.S. Marine Corps land-based service as the SBD-1, of which 57 were built with one trainable and two fixed 7.62-mm (0.3-in) machine guns. The 87 SBD-2s had greater fuel capacity and revised offensive armament. Next came the 584 SBD-3s which introduced the R-1820-52 engine, a bulletproof windscreen, armour protection, self-sealing fuel tanks of greater capacity, and the definitive machine gun armament of two 12.7-mm (0.5-in) fixed guns and two 7.62-mm (0.3-in) trainable guns. The 780 SBD-4s had a revised electrical system. The 3,025

SBD-5s had the 895-kW (1,200-hp) R-1820-60 engine and greater ammunition capacity. The 451 examples of the final SBD-6 had the yet more powerful R-1820-66 engine and increased fuel capacity.

Subvariants of this series were the SBD-1P, SBD-2P and SBD-3P photo-reconnaissance aircraft. The U.S. Army ordered an A-24 version of the SBD-3, further contracts specifying A-24A (SBD-4) and A-24B (SBD-5) aircraft, but these were not successful. The Fleet Air Arm received nine SBD-5s that were designated Dauntless DB.Mk I but not used operationally.

DOUGLAS SBD-5 DAUNTLESS
Role: Naval carrierborne dive bomber
Crew/Accommodation: Two
Power Plant: One 1,200 hp Wright R-1820-60 Cyclone air-cooled radial
Dimensions: Span 12.66 m (41.54 ft); length 10.09 m (33.1 ft); wing area 30.19 m² (325 sq ft)
Weights: Empty 2,905 kg (6,404 lb); MTOW 4,853 kg (10,700 lb)
Performance: Maximum speed 410 km/h (255 mph) at 4,265 m (14,000 ft); operational ceiling 7,780 m (25,530 ft); range 1,795 km (1,115 miles) with 726 kg (1,600 lb) bombload
Load: Two .5 inch and two .303 inch machine guns, plus up to 1,021 kg (2,250 lb) of bombs

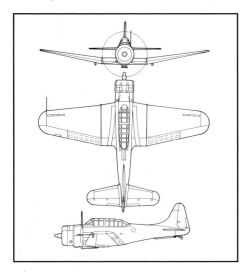

SBD-5 Dauntless

Douglas SBD Dauntless

NORTH AMERICAN B-25 MITCHELL (U.S.A.)

B-25J Mitchell

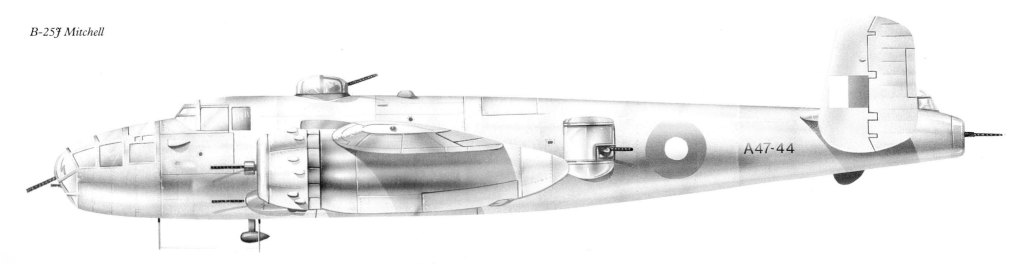

Immortalized as the mount of Doolittle's Tokyo Raiders when flown off the deck of USS *Hornet* in April 1942, the NA-40 was designed to meet a U.S. Army requirement for a twin-engined attack bomber, and emerged for its first flight in January 1939 as a shoulder-wing monoplane with tricycle landing gear and 820-kW (1,100-hp) Pratt & Whitney R-1830-S6C3-G radials that were soon

replaced by 969-kW (1,300-hp) Wright GR-2600-A71 radials. The R-2600 was retained throughout the rest of the type's 9,816-aircraft production run. Further development produced the NA-62 design with the wing lowered to the mid-position, the fuselage widened for side-by-side pilot seating, the crew increased from three to five, greater offensive and defensive armament, and 1268-kW (1,700-hp) R-2600-9 engines. In this form the type entered production as the B-25, and the first of 24 such aircraft flew in August 1940.

Development models produced in

small numbers were the B-25A (40 with armour and self-sealing fuel tanks) and B-25B (119 with power-operated dorsal and ventral turrets but with the tail gun position removed). The major production models began with the B-25C; 1,625 of this improved version were built with an autopilot, provision for an underfuselage torpedo, underwing racks for eight 113-kg (250-lb) bombs and, in some aircraft, four 12.7-mm (0.5-in) machine guns on the fuselage sides to fire directly forward. The 2,290 B-25Ds were similar but from a different production

line. A few experimental versions intervened, and the next series-built models were the B-25G (405 with a 75-mm/2.95-in nose gun) and similar B-25H (1,000 with the 75-mm gun and between 14 and 18 12.7-mm machine-guns).

The final production version was the B-25J (4,390 with R-2600-92 radials and 12 12.7-mm machine-guns). Other variants included in the total were the F-10 reconnaissance, the AT-25 and TB-25 trainers, together with the PBJ versions, the last provided for the U.S. Navy.

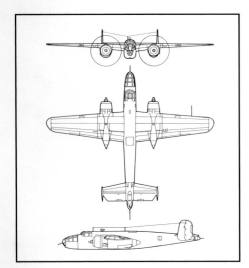

North American B-25A Mitchell

NORTH AMERICAN B-25C MITCHELL
Role: Medium bomber
Crew/Accommodation: Five/six
Power Plant: Two 1,700-hp Wright R-2600-19 Cyclone air-cooled radials
Dimensions: Span 20.6 m (67.58 ft); length 16.13 m (52.92 ft); wing area 56.67 m² (610 sq ft)
Weights: Empty 9,208 kg (20,300 lb); MTOW 15,422 kg (34,000 lb)
Performance: Maximum speed 457 km/h (284 mph) at 4,572 m (15,000 ft); operational ceiling 6,041 m (21,200 ft); range 2,414 km (1,500 miles) with full bombload
Load: Four .5-inch machine guns, plus up to 1,361 kg (3,000 lb) of bombs

North American B-25J Mitchell

DOUGLAS DB-7/A-20 HAVOC Series (U.S.A.)

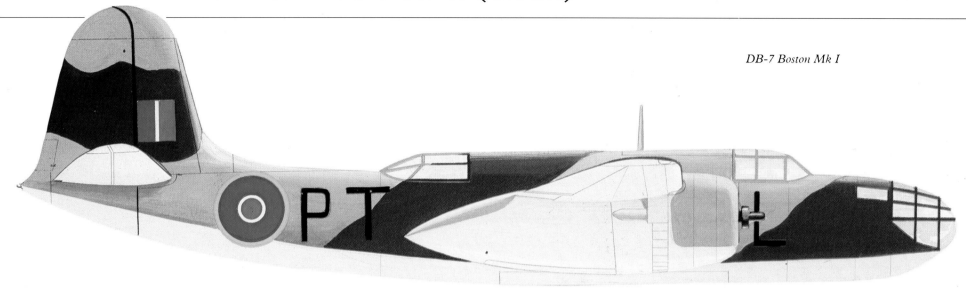

DB-7 Boston Mk I

The Model 7 was a basic twin-engined light bomber design that was evolved as a private venture and then went through a number of important forms during the course of an extensive production programme that saw the delivery of 7,478 aircraft in World War II up to September 1944. The type originated as a possible replacement for the U.S. Army's current generation of single-engined attack aircraft, and first flew as the Model 7B in October 1938 with 820-kW (1,100-hp) Pratt & Whitney R-1830 radials in place of the 336-kW (450-hp) engines of the originally

proposed Model 7A. Initial orders came from France for a Douglas Bomber 7 (DB-7) variant with 895-kW (1,200-hp) R-1830-S3C4-G engines and a deeper fuselage, followed by the improved DB-7A with 1119-kW (1,500-hp) Wright R-2600-A5B engines.

Most of these aircraft were delivered to the U.K. after the fall of France, and were placed in service with the name Boston Mks I and II, though several were converted to Havoc radar-equipped night-fighters. A redesigned DB-7B bomber variant with larger vertical tail surfaces and

British equipment became the Boston Mk III, and the same basic type was ordered by the U.S. Army as the A-20 Havoc. The latter were used mainly as reconnaissance aircraft, though a batch was converted to P-70 night fighter configuration. Thereafter the U.S. Army accepted large numbers of the A-20A and subsequent variants up to the A-20K with more power, heavier armament, and improved equipment. Many of these passed to the RAF and other British Commonwealth Air Forces in variants

up to the Boston Mk V. The steady increases in engine power maintained the performance of these types despite their greater weights and warloads. In addition to the Western Allies, the U.S.S.R. operated comparatively large numbers of the series received under Lend-Lease and often fitted with locally modified armament.

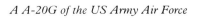

A A-20G of the US Army Air Force

DOUGLAS A-20B HAVOC
Role: Light day bomber
Crew/Accommodation: Three
Power Plant: Two 1,600 hp Wright R-2600-11 Double Cyclone air-cooled radials
Dimensions: Span 18.69 m (61.33 ft); length 14.48 m (47.5 ft); wing area 43.1 m² (464 sq ft)
Weights: Empty 6,727 kg (14,830 lb); MTOW 10,796 kg (23,800 lb)
Performance: Maximum speed 563 km/h (350 mph) at 3,658 (12,000 ft); operational ceiling 8,717 m (28,600 ft); range 1,328 km (825 miles) with 454 kg (1,000 lb) of bombs
Load: Three .5 inch and one or three .303 inch machine guns, plus to 1,089 kg (2,400 lb) of bombs

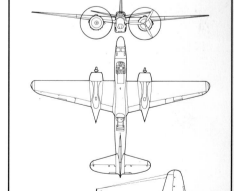

Douglas A-20J Havoc

23

PETLYAKOV Pe-2 (U.S.S.R.)

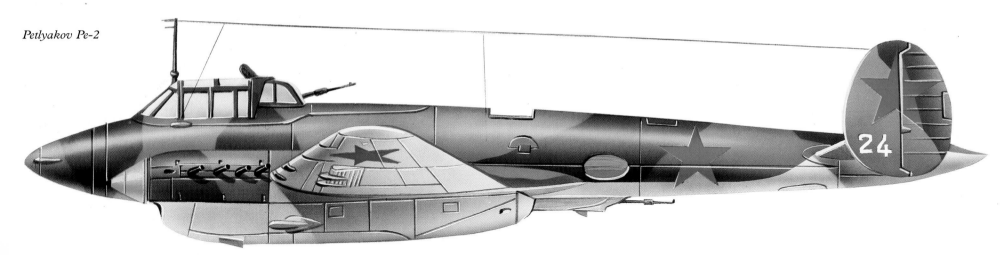

Petlyakov Pe-2

The Pe-2 was one of the U.S.S.R.'s most important tactical aircraft of World War II, and resulted from the VI-100 high-altitude fighter prototype with the 783-kW (1,050-hp) Klimov M-105 inlines. The planned role was then changed to dive-bombing, resulting in the PB-100 design for a dive-bomber with a crew of three rather than two, dive-brakes and other modifications including provision of a bomb aimer's position and elimination

of the pressure cabin. The type was of all-metal construction and a thoroughly modern concept with a cantilever low-set wing, endplate vertical tail surfaces, a circular-section fuselage, and retractable tailwheel landing gear. The aircraft entered service in November 1940 as the Pe-2 with two 902-kW (1,210-hp) VK-105RF engines, and when production ended early in 1945 some 11,427 aircraft of the series had been built.

The versatility of the type is attested by the development and production of variants intended for the bombing, reconnaissance, bomber destroyer, night fighter and conversion trainer roles. In addition to the baseline Pe-2, the main variants were the Pe-2R photo-reconnaissance type with cameras and greater fuel capacity, the Pe-2UT dual-control trainer with a revised cockpit enclosure over tandem seats, and the Pe-3 multi-role fighter, of which some 500 were built as 200 Pe-3 bomber destroyers and 300 Pe-3bis night fighters; the Pe-3 had the fixed nose

armament of two 20-mm cannon, two 12.7-mm (0.5-in) and two 7.62-mm (0.3-in) machine guns plus one 12.7-mm gun in the dorsal turret, while the Pe-3bis entered production with a nose armament of one 20-mm cannon, one 12.7-mm machine gun and three 7.62-mm machine guns but ended with two 20-mm cannon, two 12.7-mm guns and two 7.62-mm guns.

Petlyakov Pe-2

PETLYAKOV Pe-2
Role: Dive bomber
Crew/Accommodation: Three/four
Power Plant: Two 1,100 hp Klimov M-105R water-cooled inlines
Dimensions: Span 17.16 m (56.23 ft); length 12.66 m (41,54 ft); wing area 40.5 m² (435.9 sq ft)
Weights: Empty 5,876 kg (12,954 lb); MTOW 8,496 kg (18,730 lb)
Performance: Maximum speed 540 km/h (336 mph) at 5,000 m (16,404 ft); operational ceiling 8,800 m (28,871 ft); range 1,500 km (932 miles)
Load: One 12.7 mm and two 7.62 mm machine guns, plus up to 1,200 kg (2,646 lb) of bombs

Petlyakov Pe-2

de HAVILLAND D.H.98 MOSQUITO (United Kingdom)

Mosquito B.Mk VI

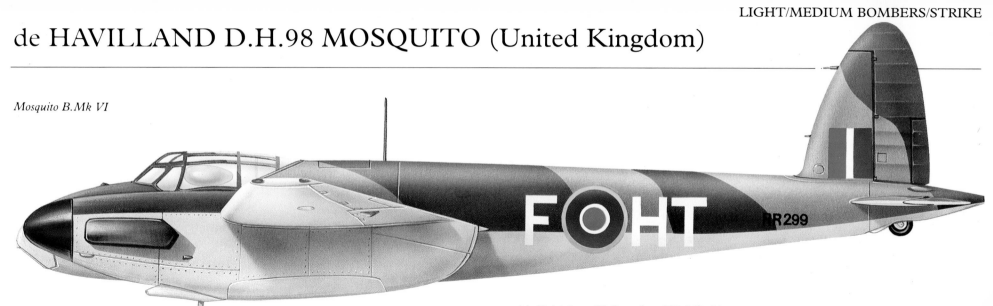

Perhaps the most versatile warplane of World War II and certainly one of the classic warplanes of all time, the 7,785 Mosquitoes began from a private venture based on the company's composite plywood/balsa construction principal. It was planned as a high-performance but unarmed light bomber. The Mk I prototype flew in November 1940. Photographic reconnaissance, fighter, trainer and bomber variants followed.

The PR versions were the Mosquito PR.Mk IV with four cameras, PR.Mk VIII with two-stage Merlins, PR.Mk IX with greater fuel capacity, PR.Mk XVI with cockpit pressurization,

PR.Mk 32 based on the NF.Mk XV, PR.Mk 34 with extra fuel in a bomb bay 'bulge', PR.Mk 40 Australian development of the FB.Mk 40, and PR.Mk 41 version of the PR.Mk 40 with two-stage engines.

The fighters were the Mosquito NF.Mk II night fighter, FB.Mk VI fighter-bomber with bombs and underwing rockets, NF.Mk XII and XIII with improved radar, NF. Mk XV conversion of the B. Mk IV for high-altitude interception, NF.Mk XVII conversion of the NF.Mk II with U.S. radar, FB.Mk XVIII anti-ship conversion or the FB.Mk VI with a 57-mm gun and rockets, NF.Mk XIX

with British or U.S. radar, FB.Mk 21 Canadian-built FB.Mk VI, FB.Mk 26 version of the FB.Mk 21 with Packard-built Merlin engines, NF.Mk 30 high-altitude model with two-stage Merlins, TR.Mk 33 naval torpedo fighter, NF.Mk 36 higher-altitude equivalent to the NF.Mk 30, TR.Mk 37 version of the TR.Mk 33 with British radar, and FB.Mk 40 Australian-built equivalent of the FB.Mk VI.

The trainer versions were the Mosquito T.Mk III, T.Mk 22 Canadian-built equivalent to the T.Mk III, T.Mk 27 version of the T.Mk 22 with Packard-built engines, T.Mk 29 conversion of the FB.Mk 26,

and T.Mk 43 Australian-built equivalent to the T.Mk III.

The bomber versions were the basic Mosquito B.Mk IV, B.Mk VII Canadian-built type with underwing hardpoints, B.Mk IX high-altitude type with a single 1814-kg (4,000-lb) bomb, B.Mk XVI development of the B.Mk IX with pressurized cockpit, B.Mk 20 B.Mk 25 version of the B.Mk 20 and B.Mk 35 long-range high-altitude model.

---

de HAVILLAND D.H.98 MOSQUITO NF. Mk 36
Role: Night/all-weather fighter
Crew/Accommodation: Two
Power Plant: Two 1,690 hp Rolls-Royce Merlin 113 water-cooled inlines
Dimensions: Span 16.51 m (54.17 ft); length 12.34 m (40.5 ft); wing area 42.18 m² (454 sq ft)
Weights: Empty 7,257 kg (16,000 lb); MTOW 9,707 kg (21,400 lb)
Performance: Maximum speed 650 km/h (404 mph) at 8,717 m (28,600 ft); operational ceiling 10,972 m (36,000 ft); range 2,704 km (1,680 miles)
Load: Four 20 mm cannon (interception guided by AI Mk 10 radar)

This is a de Havilland Mosquito T.Mk III trainer of the Royal Air Force

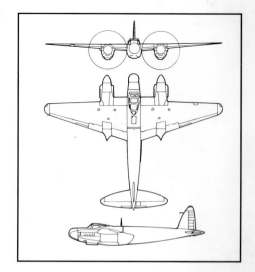

Mosquito NF.Mk 36

ILYUSHIN Il-2 (U.S.S.R.)

Ilyushin Il-2

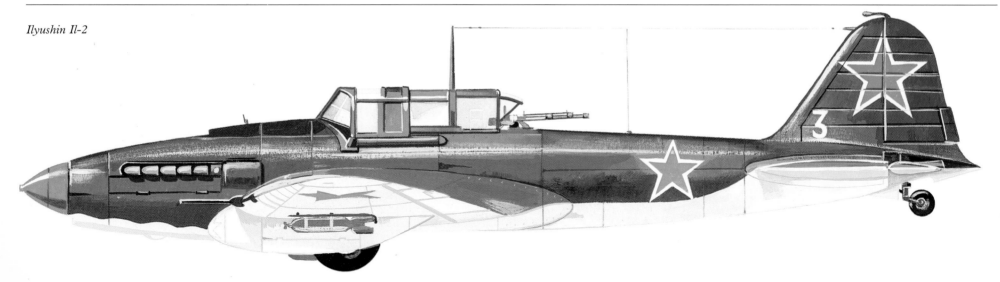

The Il-2 was probably the finest ground-attack aircraft of World War II and was built to the extent of some 36,165 aircraft. The type began life as the TsKB-55 (alternatively BSh-2 or DBSh) two-seat prototype that first flew in December 1939 with the 1007-kW (1,350-hp) Mikulin AM-35 inline engine. Flight tests indicated that the type was too heavy because of its massive armour 'bath' structural core,

so the basic design was developed into the single-seat TsKB-57 that flew in October 1940 with a 1268-kW (1,700-hp) Mikulin AM-38 inline. This entered production as the single-seat BSh-2, a designation that was altered to Il-2 during April 1941, and by August production had risen to some 300 aircraft per month.

Early operations confirmed the design bureau's initial objections to the removal of the TsKB-55's rear gunner, for the Il-2 was found to be especially vulnerable to rear attack. The Il-2 was therefore refined as the

Il-2M with the cockpit extended aft for a rear gunner equipped with a 12.7-mm (0.5-in) machine gun but separated from the pilot by a fuel tank. The original two wing-mounted 20-mm cannon were replaced by 23-mm weapons offering greater armour-penetration capability, and provision was made for the eight 82-mm (3.2-in) rockets to be replaced by four 132-mm (5.2-in) weapons. Later the type was also produced in the aerodynamically improved Il-2 Type 3 version with a 1320-kW (1,770-hp) engine, a refined canopy and faster-

acting doors for the bomb cells in the wings that carried 200 2.5-kg (5.51-lb) anti-tank bomblets. There was also an Il-2 Type 3M variant with further aerodynamic refinement, and a fixed forward-firing armament of two 37-mm cannon complemented by up to 32 82-mm (1 in) rockets on a two-stage zero-length installation. Other Il-2 versions were the Il-2T torpedo bomber with one 533-mm (21-in) torpedo under the fuselage and the Il-2U tandem-seat trainer. Production ended in late 1944 to allow for the much improved Il-10.

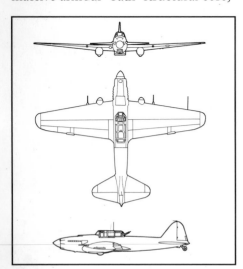

ILYUSIHN Il-2M
Role: Strike/close air support
Crew/Accommodation: Two
Power Plant: One 1,700 hp AM-38F water-cooled inline
Dimensions: Span 14.6 m (47.9 ft); length 11.6 m (38.06 ft); wing area 38.5 m² (414.41 sq ft)
Weights: Empty 4,525 kg (9,976 lb); MTOW 6,360 kg (14,021 lb)
Performance: Maximum speed 404 km/h (251 mph) at 1,500 m (4,921 ft); operational ceiling 6,000 m (19,685 ft); range 765 km (475 miles) with full warload
Load: Two 23 mm cannon and two 7.62 mm machine guns, plus up to 600 kg (1,321 lb) of bombs or anti-armour rockets

Ilyushin Il-2 Type 3M

MARTIN B-26 MARAUDER (U.S.A.)

B-26F Marauder

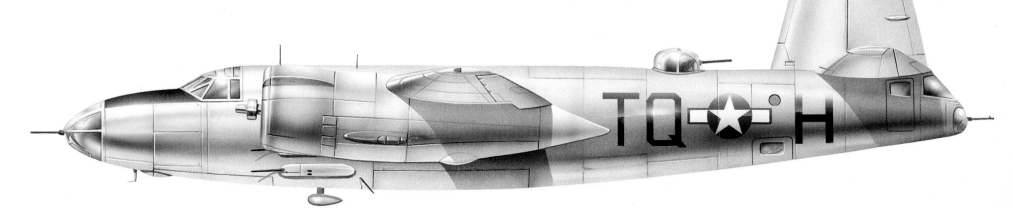

The Marauder was designed to meet a particularly difficult specification issued in 1939 by the U.S. Army Air Corps for a high-performance medium bomber, and was ordered 'off the drawing board' straight into production without any prototype or even pre-production aircraft. The first B-26 flew in November 1940 with two 1380-kW (1,850-hp) Pratt & Whitney R-2800-5 radials as a highly streamlined mid-wing monoplane with tricycle landing gear. The type was able to deliver the required performance, but because of the high wing loading low-speed handling was poor, resulting in a spate of accidents.

Total production was 4,708 aircraft, and in addition to the 201 B-26s the main variants were the B-26A (139 aircraft) with 1380-kW (1,850-hp) R-2800-9 or -39 engines, greater fuel capacity and provision for an underfuselage torpedo, the B-26C (1,883) with 1491-kW (2,000-hp) R-2800-41 engines and, from the 642nd aircraft, a wing increased in span by 1.83 m (6 ft 0 in) as a means of reducing wing loading, though this was negated by inevitably increased weight, the B-26C (1,210) generally similar to the B-26B but from a different production line, the B-26F (300) which introduced a higher wing incidence angle to improve field performance, and the B-26G (893) generally similar to the B-26F. There were two target tug-gunnery trainer variants produced by converting bombers as 208 AT-23As (later TB-26Bs) and 375 AT-23Bs (later TB-26Cs); 225 of the latter were transferred to the U.S. Navy as JM-1s. There was also the new-build TB-26G crew trainer, and 47 of these 57 aircraft were transferred to the U.S. Navy as JM-2s. Comparatively large numbers of several models were used by the British and, to a lesser extent, the French and South Africans.

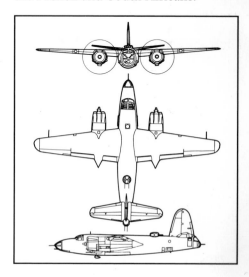

Martin B-26G Marauder

This Martin B-26B Marauder shows evidence of protracted services

MARTIN B-26B MARAUDER
Role: Medium bomber
Crew/Accommodation: Seven
Power Plant: Two 2,000 hp Pratt & Whitney R-2800-41 Double Wasp air-cooled radials
Dimensions: Span 21.64 m (71 ft); length 17.75 m (58.25 ft); wing area 61.13 m² (658 sq ft)
Weights: Empty 10,660 kg (23,500 lb); MTOW 17,328 kg (38,200 lb)
Performance: Maximum speed 454 km/h (282 mph) at 4,572 m (15,000 ft); operational ceiling 4,572+ m (15,000+ ft); range 1,086 km (675 miles) with maximum bombload
Load: Twelve .5 inch machine guns, plus up to 1,815 kg (4,000 lb) of internally carried bombs, or one externally carried torpedo

CURTISS SB2C HELLDIVER (U.S.A.)

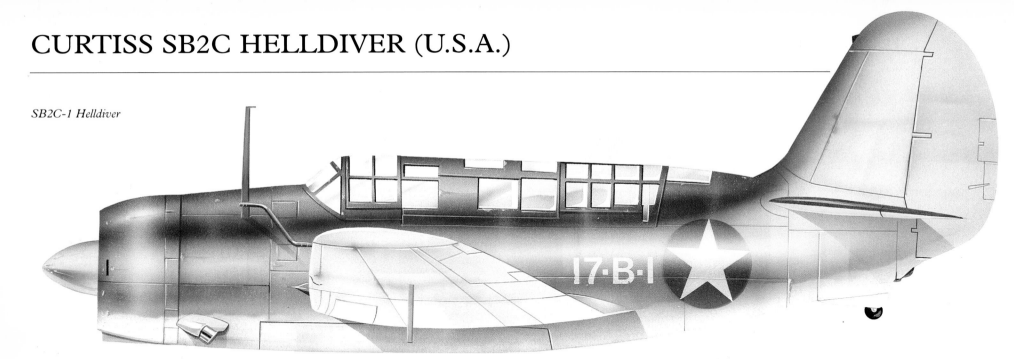

SB2C-1 Helldiver

The SB2C was the third Curtiss design to bear the name Helldiver, the first two having been the F8C/O2C biplanes of the early 1930s and SBC biplane of the late 1930s. The Model 84 (or SB2C) monoplane was designed in competition to the Brewster XSB2A Buccaneer as successor to the Model 77 (or SBC) biplane in the carrierborne scout bomber/dive bomber role. The type was designed as a substantial all-metal monoplane of the low-wing variety with retractable tailwheel landing gear (complete with arrester hook), a substantial tail unit, and a deep oval-section fuselage characterized by extensive glazing over the rear compartment. The X2B2C-1 prototype flew in December 1940 but was lost in an accident only a short time later. The U.S. Navy had considerable faith in the type,

however, and large-scale production had already been authorized to launch a programme that saw the eventual delivery of 7,200 aircraft. But because of the need to co-develop an A-25A version for the U.S. Army, the first SB2C-1 production aeroplane with the 1268-kW (1,700-hp) Wright R-2600-8 Cyclone 14 radial did not emerge until June 1942. The A-25A in fact entered only the most limited of army service, and the majority of the army's aircraft were reassigned to the U.S. Marine Corps in the land-based

role with the designation SB2C-1A.

Other variants were the SB2C-1C with the four wing-mounted 12.7-mm (0.5-in) machine guns replaced by two 20-mm cannon, the SB2C-3 with the 1417-kW (1,900-hp) R-2600-20 engine, the SB2C-4 with underwing bomb/rocket racks, the radar-fitted SB2C-4E, and the SB2C-5 with greater fuel capacity. Similar versions were built by Fairchild and Canadian Car & Foundry with the basic designation SBF and SBW respectively.

CURTISS SB2C-5 HELLDIVER
Role: Naval carrierborne bomber/reconnaissance
Crew/Accommodation: Two
Power Plant: One 1,900-hp Wright R-2600-20 Double Cyclone air-cooled radial
Dimensions: Span 15.15 m (49.75 ft); length 11.17 m (36.66 ft); wing area 39.2 m² (422 sq ft)
Weights: Empty 4,799 kg (10,580 lb); MTOW 7,388 kg (16,287 lb)
Performance: Maximum speed 418 km/h (260 mph) at 4,907 m (16,100 ft); operational ceiling 8,047 m (26,400 ft); range 1,875 km (1,165 miles) with 454 kg (1,000 lb) bombload
Load: Two 20-mm cannon and two .303-inch machine guns, plus up to 907 kg (2,000 lb) of bombs

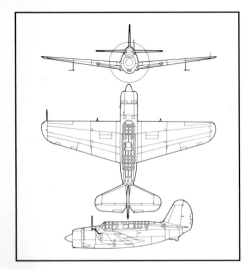

SB2C-1C Helldiver

Curtiss SB2C Helldiver

GRUMMAN TBF AVENGER (U.S.A.)

TBF-1 Avenger

Despite a disastrous combat debut in which five out of six aircraft were lost, the TBF Avenger was a decisive warplane of World War II, and may rightly be regarded as the Allies' premier carrierborne torpedo bomber. The TBF resulted from a 1940 requirement for a successor to the Douglas TBD Devastator. Orders were placed for two Vought XTBU-1 prototype in addition to the two XTBF-1s, and the Grumman type first flew in August 1941 on the power of the 1268-kW (1,700-hp) Wright R-

2600-8 Cyclone radial. The type was of typical Grumman design and construction, and despite the fact that it was the company's first essay in the field of carrierborne torpedo bombers, the Avenger proved itself a thoroughbred and immensely strong.

The type was ordered into production as the TBF-1 or, with two additional heavy machine-guns in the wings plus provision for drop tanks, TBF-1C; production totalled 2,291 aircraft. The Royal Navy also received the type as the Tarpon Mk I, later

changed to Avenger Mk I. The Eastern Aircraft Division of General Motors was also brought into the programme to produce similar models as 550 TBM-1s and 2,336 TBM-1Cs (Avenger Mk IIs), and the only major development was the TBM-3. Eastern produced 4,657 of this model, which had been pioneered as the XTBF-3 with the 1417-kW (1,900-hp) R-2600-219 engine and strengthened wings for the carriage of drop tanks or rockets.

Many of the aircraft were delivered without the initial model's heavy power-operated dorsal turret.

Late in World War II and after the war, the series was diversified into a host of other roles, each indicated by a special suffix, such as photo-reconnaissance, early warning, electronic warfare, anti-submarine search/attack, transport, and target towing. Total production was 9,839 aircraft.

A version of the Grumman TBF Avenger, the TBM, built by General Motors

---

GRUMMAN TBF-1 AVENGER
Role: Naval carrierborne strike
Crew/Accommodation: Three
Power Plant: One 1,700 hp Wright R-2600-8 Double Cyclone air-cooled radial
Dimensions: Span 16.51 m (54.16 ft); length 12.23 m (40.125 ft); wing area 45.52 m² (490 sq ft)
Weights: Empty 4,572 kg (10,080 lb); MTOW 7,214 kg (15,905 lb)
Performance: Maximum speed 436 km/h (271 mph) at 3,658 m (12,000 ft); operational ceiling 6,828 m (22,400 ft); range 1,955 km (1,215 miles) with torpedo
Load: One .5 inch and two .303 inch machine guns, plus up to 726 kg (1,600 lb) of internally-stowed torpedo or bombs

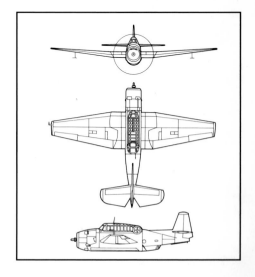

Grumman TBF-1 Avenger

MITSUBISHI Ki-67 HIRYU 'PEGGY' (Japan)

Ki-67-I Type 4 'Peggy'

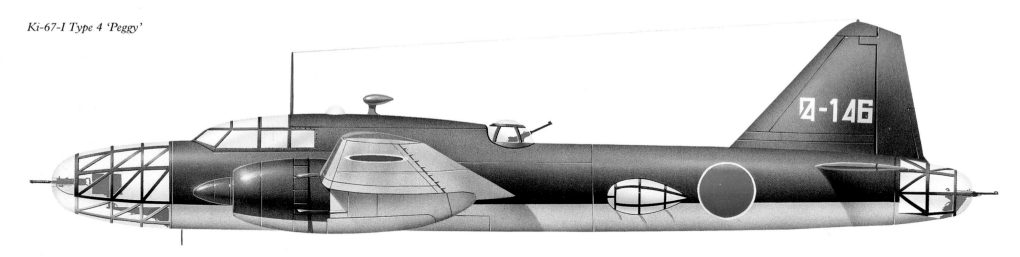

In February 1941, Mitsubishi received instructions from the Imperial Japanese Army Air Force to design a tactical heavy bomber, and the company responded with a type that secured good performance and agility through the typically Japanese defects of minimal protection (armour and self-sealing fuel tanks) combined with a lightweight structure that was little suited to sustain battle damage.

The first of 19 Ki-67 prototypes and pre-production aircraft flew in December 1942 with two 1417-kW (1,900-hp) Mitsubishi Ha-104 radials. Production was delayed as the Japanese army considered a whole range of derivatives based on this high-performance basic aircraft, but in December 1943, the army belatedly decided to concentrate on just a single heavy bomber type capable of the level and torpedo bombing roles. The type entered production with the company designation Ki-67-I and entered service as the Army Type 4 Heavy Bomber Model 1 Hiryu (Flying Dragon). Only 679 of these effective aircraft were built, all but the first 159 having provision for an underfuselage rack carrying one torpedo to give the type an anti-ship capability. Many were converted as three-seat Ki-67-I KAI *kamikaze* aircraft with the defensive gun turrets removed and provision made for two 800-kg (1,764-lb) bombs or 2900 kg (6,393 lb) of explosives. Further production was to have been of the Ki-67-II version with two 1789-kW (2,400-hp) Mitsubishi Ha-214 radials, however, the only other production was in fact of the Ki-109 heavy fighter variant. This type was armed with a 75-mm (2.95-in) nose gun in the bomber destroyer role, and production totalled just 22 aircraft before the end of World War II. The Ki-67 was known to the Allies as the 'Peggy', however the Ki-109 received no reporting name.

MITSUBISHI Ki-67-1 OTSU HIRYU 'PEGGY'
Role: Bomber
Crew/Accommodation: Eight
Power Plant: Two 1,900-hp Mitsubishi Ha-104 air-cooled radials
Dimensions: Span 22.5 m (73.82 ft); length 18.7 m (61.35 ft); wing area 65.85 m² (708.8 sq ft)
Weights: Empty 8,649 kg (19,068 lb); MTOW 13,765 kg (30,347 lb)
Performance: Maximum speed 537 km/h (334 mph) at 6,090 m (19,980 ft); operational ceiling 9,470 m (31,070 ft); range 2,800 km (1,740 miles) with 500 kg (1,102 lb) bombload
Load: One 20-mm cannon and four 12.7-mm machine guns, plus up to 1,080 kg (2,359 lb) of ordnance, including one heavyweight torpedo

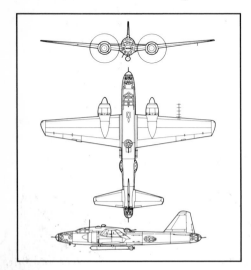

Mitsubishi Ki-67-I Hiryu

Mitsubishi Ki-67-iB

DOUGLAS A-1 SKYRAIDER (U.S.A.)

A-1B Skyraider

The massive single-seat Skyraider was designed as a carrierborne dive- and torpedo-bomber, and the first of 25 XBT2D-1 Destroyer II prototype and service test aircraft flew in March 1945. The capabilities of the new aircraft were so impressive that large-scale production was ordered and it proved an invaluable U.S. tool in the Korean and Vietnam Wars.

The type went through a number of major marks, the most significant being the 242 AD-1s with the 1864-kW (2,500-hp) R-3350-24W radial and an armament of two 20-mm cannon plus 3629 kg (8,000 lb) of disposable stores, the 156 improved AD-2s with greater fuel capacity and other modifications, the 125 AD-3s with a redesigned canopy and longer-stroke landing gear as well as other improvements, the 372 AD-4s with the 2014-kW (2,700-hp) R-3350-26WA and an autopilot, the 165 nuclear-capable AD-4Bs with four 20-mm cannon, the 212 AD-5 anti-submarine search and attack aircraft with a widened fuselage for a side-by-side crew of two, the 713 examples of the AD-6 improved version of the AD-4B with equipment for highly accurate low-level bombing, and the 72 examples of the AD-7 version of the AD-6 with the R-3350-26WB engine and strengthened structure.

From 1962 all surviving aircraft were redesignated in the A-1 sequence. The Skyraider's large fuselage and greater load-carrying capability also commended the type for adaptation to other roles, and these roles were generally indicated by a letter suffix to the final number of the designation; E indicated anti-submarine search with radar under the port wing, N three-seat night attack, Q two-seat electronic counter-measures, S anti-submarine attack in concert with an E type, and W three/four-seat airborne early warning with radar in an underfuselage radome. Total production was 3,180 aircraft up to 1957, and from 1962 the series was redesignated in the A-1 series.

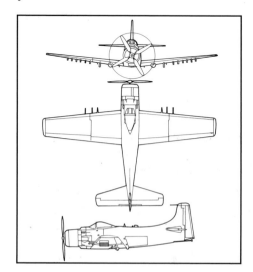

Douglas A-1J Skyraider

DOUGLAS AD-1 SKYRAIDER
Role: Naval carrierborne strike
Crew/Accommodation: One
Power Plant: One 2,500 hp Wright R-3350-24W air-cooled radial
Dimensions: Span 15.24 m (50.02 ft); length 12 m (39.35 ft); wing area 37.19 m² (400.3 sq ft)
Weights: Empty 4,749 kg (10,470 lb); MTOW 8,178 kg (18,030 lb)
Performance: Maximum speed 517 km/h (321 mph) at 5,580 m (18,300 ft); operational ceiling 7,925 m (26,000 ft); range 2,500 km (1,554 miles)
Load: Two 20 mm cannon, plus up to 2,722 kg (6,000 lb) of weapons

A Douglas A-1H Skyraider with the markings of the South Vietnamese Air Force

ENGLISH ELECTRIC CANBERRA AND MARTIN B-57 (United Kingdom)

Canberra B(I).Mk 6

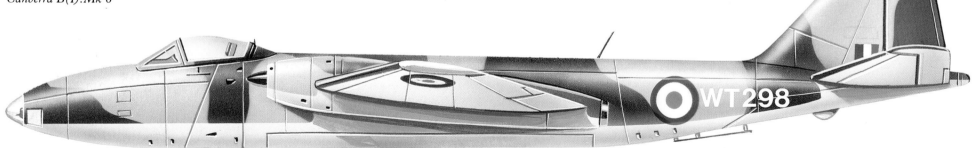

The Canberra was planned as a nuclear-capable medium bomber with turbojet engines, and as a high-altitude type it was designed round a large wing and a crew of two using a radar bombing system. It matured as a medium/high-altitude type with optical bomb aiming by a third crew member and first flew in May 1949. Canberra was the first jet bomber produced in Britain, the RAF's first jet bomber, and the first aircraft in history to cross the Atlantic twice in a single day (1952). Its great development potential ensured that the type enjoyed a long first-line

career as well as diversification into other roles. The main bomber stream began with the Canberra B.Mk 2 powered by 2,948-kg (6,500-lb) Avon RA.3 Mk 101 turbojets, and then advanced to the B.Mk 6 with greater fuel capacity and 3,357-kg (7,400-lb) thrust Avon Mk 109s, the B.Mk 15 conversion of the B.Mk 6 with underwing hardpoints, the B.Mk 16 improved B.Mk 15, and the B.Mk 20 Australian-built B.Mk 6; there were also many export versions. The intruder/interdictor series began with the Canberra B(I).Mk 6 version of the B.Mk 6 with underwing bombs and a ventral cannon pack, and continued with the B(I).Mk 8 multi-role version; there were also several export versions. The reconnaissance models began with the Canberra

PR.Mk 3 based on the B.Mk 2, and then moved through variants including the PR.Mk 7 equivalent of the B.Mk 6, and the PR.Mk 9 high-altitude model with increased span, extended centre-section chord, and 4,990-kg (11,000-lb) thrust Avon Mk 206s; there were also a few export models. Other streams included trainer, target tug and remotely controlled target drone models. The last surviving Canberras were mostly of reconnaissance and electronic warfare types, but not exclusively. The importance of the Canberra is also attested by the fact that it became the first non-U.S. type to be manufactured under licence in the U.S. after World War II. This variant was the Martin B-57, the first version of which was the B-57A with Wright J65-W-1 (licence-built Armstrong Siddeley Sapphire) turbojets.

The main production model was the B-57B, an extensively adapted night intruder with two seats in tandem and a fixed armament of four 20-mm cannon plus eight 12.7-mm (0.5-in) machine-guns as well as the standard bomb bay and underwing loads. Other variants were the B-57C dual-control version of the B-57B, and the B-57E target-tug version of the B-57B. The aircraft were also extensively converted as RB-57 photo-reconnaissance and EB-57 electronic warfare platforms, the most radical such version being the General Dynamics-produced RB-57F with span increased to 37.19 m (122 ft 0 in) for ultra-high flight with two 8,165-kg (18,000-lb) thrust Pratt & Whitney TF33-P-11 turbofans and, in underwing nacelles, two 1,497-kg (3,300-lb) thrust Pratt & Whitney J60-P-9 turbojets.

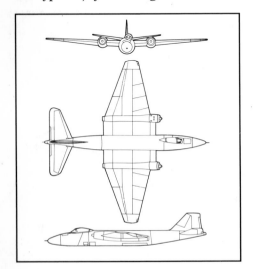

Canberra PR.Mk 9

ENGLISH ELECTRIC CANBERRA B.Mk 2
Role: Bomber reconnaissance
Crew/Accommodation: Two
Power Plant: Two 2,948 kgp (6,500 lb s.t.) Rolls-Royce Avon RA.3 Mk 101 turbojets
Dimensions: Span 19.49 m (63.96 ft); length 19.96 m (65.5 ft); wing area 89.2 m² (960 sq ft)
Weights: Empty 10,070 kg (22,200 lb); MTOW 20,865 kg (46,000 lb)
Performance: Maximum speed 917 km/h (570 mph) at 12,192 m (40,000 ft); operational ceiling 14,630 m (48,000 ft); range 4,281 km (2,660 miles)
Load: Up to 2,722 kg (6,000 lb) of ordnance all carried internally

This Argentine bomber is a English Electric Canberra B.Mk 62

TUPOLEV Tu-16 'BADGER' (U.S.S.R.)

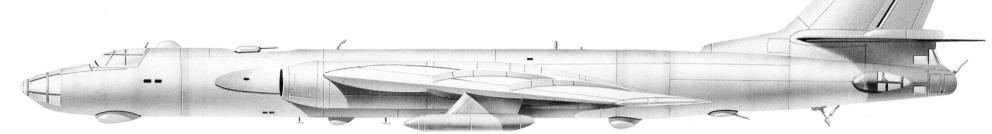

Tu-16 'Badger'

A great technical achievement in the fields of aerodynamics and structures by the Tupolev design bureau, the Tu-16 twin-jet intermediate-range strategic bomber first flew as the type 88 prototype in April 1952, with production at Kazan beginning in 1953 and later at Kuibyshev. In May 1954 nine bombers flew over Red Square and later that year the Tu-16KS missile carrier flew for the first time. By 1963, all 1,500 or thereabouts production aircraft had been delivered, although other versions followed by conversion of existing models.

The baseline 'Badger-A' bomber was originally equipped with free-fall weapons while the 'Badger-B'was developed as a launcher for anti-ship missiles, but later became a free-fall bomber. The 'Badger-C' was an anti-ship type carrying either one AS-2 'Kipper' under the fuselage or two AS-6 'Kingfish' missiles under the wings. The 'Badger-D' was an electronic and/or maritime reconnaissance platform while 'Badger-E' first appeared in 1955 as a photo-reconnaissance and electronic intelligence version. The 'Badger-F' was a conversion of 'Badger-A' for sea reconnaissance. The 'Badger-G' became a very important anti-ship and anti-radar missile carrier with two AS-5 'Kelt' or, in its 'Badger-G (Modified)' form with AS-6 'Kingfish' missiles under its wings. The 'Badger-H', 'J', 'K', and 'L' were all developed as air force or naval electronic warfare aircraft optimized for the escort and/or stand-off, locator jamming, revised locator jamming and electronic intelligence/jamming roles respectively. Many of the older aircraft were finally converted into either of two types of in-flight refuelling tanker. By 1998, the Tu-16 was out of service in Russia. However, the same basic type is produced in China as the Xi'an H-6 bomber and anti-ship missile carrier, after receipt of a licence in 1957.

Tupolev Tu-16 tanker and bomber

TUPOLEV Tu-16 'BADGER-G'
Role: Missile-carrying bomber, reconnaissance, electronic warfare
Crew/Accommodation: Six to nine dependent on mission
Power Plant: Two 8,750-kgp (19,290-lb s.t.) Mikulin AM-3M turbojets
Dimensions: Span 32.93 m (108 ft); length 34.8 m (114.2 ft); wing area 164.65 m² (1,772 sq ft)
Weights: Empty 40,000 kg (88,185 lb); MTOW 77,000 kg (169,756 lb)
Performance: Maximum speed 941 km/h (585 mph) at 11,000 m (36,090 ft); operational ceiling 12,200 m (40,026 ft); radius 2,895 km (1,800 miles) unrefuelled with full warload
Load: Three 23-mm cannon, plus up to 9,000 kg (19,842 lb) of bombs

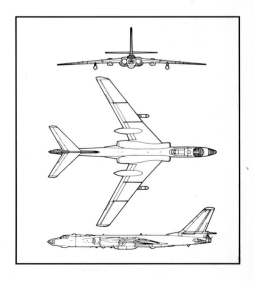

Tupolev Tu-16 'Badger-A'

33

McDONNELL DOUGLAS A-4 SKYHAWK (U.S.A.)

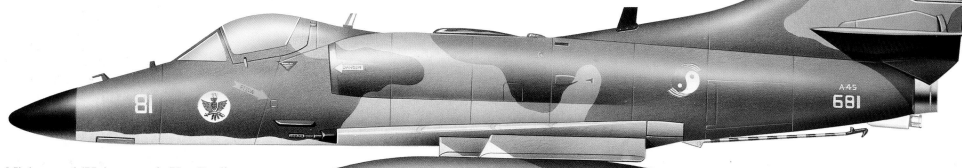

A-4S Super Skyhawk

Nicknamed 'Heinemann's Hot Rod' after its designer, the Skyhawk was conceived as a private-venture successor to the AD Skyraider. At this time the U.S. Navy envisaged a turboprop-powered machine in the role, but Douglas produced its design to offer all the specified payload/range capability in an airframe that promised higher-than-specified performance and about half the planned maximum take-off weight. The concept was sufficiently attractive for the service to order two XA4D-1 prototypes, and the first of these flew in June 1954 as a low-wing delta monoplane with integral fuel tankage

and the 3,266-kg (7,200-lb) Wright J65-W-2 version of a British turbojet, the Armstrong Siddeley Sapphire. Production deliveries began in October 1956 and continued to February 1979 for a total of 2,960 aircraft.

The first version was the A4D-1 (A-4A from 1962), of which just 19 were delivered with the 3,493-kg (7,700-lb) thrust Wright J65-W-4 and an armament of two 20-mm cannon and 2,268 kg (5,000 lb) of disposable stores. The main successor

variants were the 542 A4D-2s (A-4Bs) with more power and inflight-refuelling capability, the 638 A4D-2Ns (A-4Cs) with terrain-following radar and more power, the 494 A4D-5s (A-4Es) with the 3,856-kg (8,500-lb) thrust Pratt & Whitney J52-P-6 turbojet and two additional hardpoints for a 3,719-kg (8,200-lb) disposable load, the 146 A-4Fs with a dorsal hump for more advanced electronics, the 90 examples of the A-4H based on the A-4E for Israel with 30-mm cannon and upgraded

electronics, the 162 A-4Ms with an enlarged dorsal hump and more power, and the 117 examples of the A-4N development of the A-4M for Israel. There were a number of TA-4 trainer models, and other suffixes were used to indicate aircraft built or rebuilt for export. There is currently a considerable boom in upgraded aircraft, some (such as Argentina's refurbished A-4AR Fightinghawks) only now going back into service.

A McDonnell Douglas A-4M Skyhawk II of the VMA-324 squadron

McDONNELL DOUGLAS A-4E SKYHAWK
Role: Naval carrierborne strike
Crew/Accommodation: One
Power Plant: One 3,856-kgp (8,500-lb s.t.) Pratt & Whitney J52-P-6A turbojet
Dimensions: Span 8.38 m (27.5 ft); length 12.23 m (40.125 ft); wing area 24.16 m² (260 sq ft)
Weights: Empty 4,469 kg (9,853 lb); MTOW 11,113 kg (24,500 lb)
Performance: Maximum speed 1,083 km/h (673 mph) at sea level; operational ceiling 11,460 m (37,600 ft); range 1,865 km (1,160 miles) with 1,451-kg (3,200- lb) bombload
Load: Two 20-mm cannon, plus up to 3,719 kg (8,200 lb) of weapons

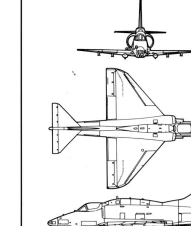

A-4N Skyhawk II

SUKHOI Su-7 'FITTER' Family (U.S.S.R.)

Su-7B 'Fitter'

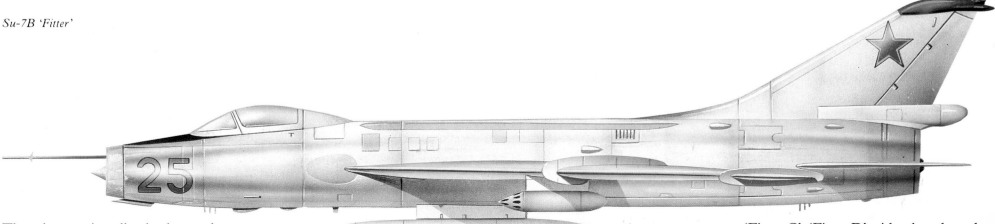

Though now virtually obsolete and no longer in Russian service, in its time the Su-7 had a superb reputation as a ground-attack fighter able to absorb practically any amount of combat damage yet still deliver its ordnance with accuracy. On the other side of the coin, however, the type was given an engine so prodigiously thirsty that at least two hardpoints were used for drop tanks rather than ordnance.

Various S-1 and S-2 prototypes flew in the mid-1950s, the latter introducing a slab tailplane, and during 1958 the Su-7 was ordered with the 9,000-kg (19,841-lb) thrust Lyulka AL-7F turbojet as the service version of the S-22 pre-production derivative of the S-2 with an area-ruled fuselage. The type was developed in steadily improved Su-7 variants, known to NATO by the reporting name 'Fitter-A', with greater power, soft-field capability and six rather than four hardpoints. This effective yet short-ranged type was then transformed into the far more potent Su-17 with variable-geometry outer wing panels. The Su-

71G prototype of 1966 confirmed that field performance and range were markedly improved. With the 10,000-kg (22,046-lb) AL7F-1 turbojet in early aircraft and the 11,200-kg (24,691-lb) thrust AL-21F-3/F-3A in later aircraft, the variable-geometry type was extensively built up to 1990 for Soviet, Warsaw Pact and allied use.

The main Soviet and Warsaw Pact models were delivered as Su-17 variants known to NATO as the

'Fitter-C', 'Fitter-D' with a lengthened nose, 'Fitter-H' with a new weapon system, and 'Fitter-K' as the most advanced version and having ten weapon pylons. The main export variant was the Su-20 with inferior electronics to the Soviet 'Fitter-C', while the Su-22 became a Third-World export model with the 11,500-kg (25,353-lb) Tumansky R-29BS-300 or later AL-21F3 turbojet and inferior electronics. The final models in Russian service were for reconnaissance, but many remain flying with other air forces.

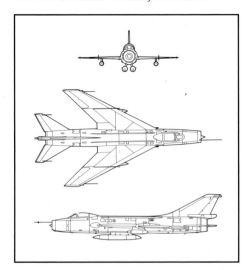

Sukhoi Su-7B 'Fitter-A'

SUKHOI Su-7BMK 'FITTER A'
Role: Strike-fighter
Crew/Accommodation: One
Power Plant: One 9,600 kgp (21,164 lb s.t.) Lyulka AL-7F-1 turbojet with reheat
Dimensions: Span 8.77 m (28.77 ft); length 16.8 m (55.12 ft); wing area 34.5 m² (371.4 sq ft)
Weights: Empty 8,616 kg (18,995 lb); MTOW 13,500 kg (29,762 lb)
Performance: Maximum speed 1,160 km/h (720 mph) Mach 0.95 at 305 m (1,000 ft); operational ceiling 13,000+ m (42,650 ft); radius 460 km (285 miles) with 1,500 kg (3,307 lb) warload
Load: Two 3 mm cannon, plus up to 2,500 kg (5,512 lb) of weapons/fuel carried externally

Sukhoi Su-7 'Fitter'

NORTH AMERICAN A-5 VIGILANTE (U.S.A.)

RA-5C Vigilante

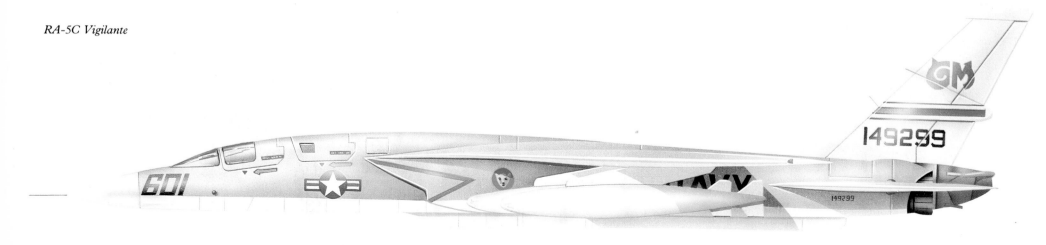

The Vigilante was designed as a Mach 2 all-weather strike aircraft to provide the U.S. Navy with a carrierborne type able to deliver strategic nuclear weapons, and the design known as the North American General Purpose Attack Weapon was ordered in the form of two YA3J-1 prototypes. The first of these flew in August 1958 with two 7326-kg (16,150-lb) thrust General Electric J79-GE-2

afterburning turbojets aspirated via the first variable-geometry inlets fitted on any operational warplane. The overall design was of great sophistication, and included wing spoilers for roll control in conjunction with differentially operating slab tailplane halves that worked in concert for pitch control. Considerable problems were caused by the design's weapon bay, which was a longitudinal tunnel that contained fuel cells as well as the nuclear weapon in a package that was ejected to the rear as the Vigilante flew

over the target.

The A3J-1 began to enter service in June 1961 with the 7711-kg (17,000-lb) thrust J79-GE-8, and just over a year later the type was redesignated A-5A. These 57 aircraft were followed by the A-5B long-range version with additional fuel in a large dorsal hump, wider-span flaps, blown leading-edge flaps, and four underwing hardpoints. Only six of this variant were built as a change in the U.S. Navy's strategic

nuclear role led to the Vigilante's adaptation for the reconnaissance role with additional tankage and cameras in the weapon bay and side-looking airborne radar in a ventral canoe fairing. Production of this RA-5C model totalled 55 with 8101-kg (17,860-lb) thrust J79-GE-10 engines and revised inlets, in addition, extra capability was provided by 59 conversions (53 A-5As and the six A-5Bs).

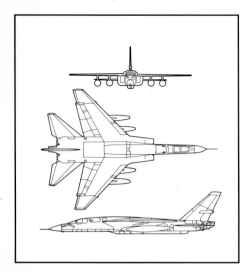

RA-5C Vigilante

NORTH AMERICAN A-5A VIGILANTE
Role: Naval carrierborne nuclear bomber
Crew/Accommodation: Two
Power Plant: Two 7,324 kgp (16,150 lb s.t.) General Electric J79-GE-2/4/8 turbojets with reheat
Dimensions: Span 16.15 m (53 ft); length 23.11 m (75.83 ft); wing area 71.45 m² (769 sq ft)
Weights: Empty 17,009 kg (37,498 lb); MTOW 36.287 kg (80,000 lb)
Performance: Maximum speed 2,229 km/h (1,203 knots) Mach 2.1 at 12.192 m (40,000 ft); operational ceiling 14,326 m (47,000 ft); range 3,862 km (2,084 naut. miles) with nuclear weapons
Load: One multi-megaton warhead class nuclear weapon

The North American RA-5C Vigilante

BLACKBURN BUCCANEER (United Kingdom)

Buccaneer S.Mk 2B

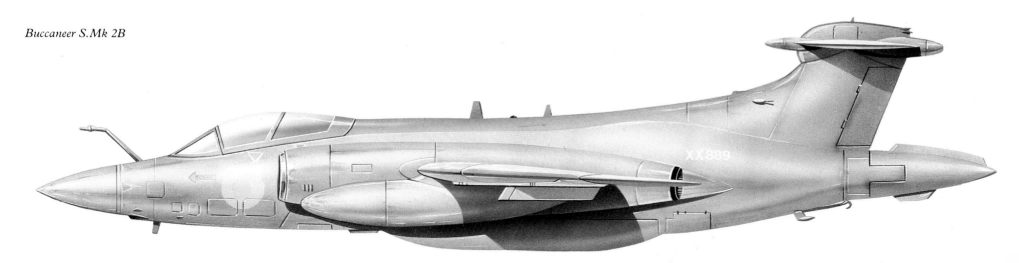

This superb aircraft was planned as a B-103 to meet the NA.39 requirement for a carrierborne low-level transonic strike warplane, and was designed with a boundary layer control system for the wings and tailplane, an area-ruled fuselage, a sizeable weapon bay with a rotary door carrying the main weapons, and a vertically split tail cone that could be opened into larger-area air brakes. The prototype was the first of 20 pre-production aircraft, and first flew in April 1958 with two 3,175-kg (7,000-lb) thrust de Havilland Gyron Junior DGJ. 1 turbojets.

Forty Buccaneer S.Mk 1s were ordered with the 3,221-kg (7,100-lb) thrust Gyron Junior 101, and these began to enter service in July 1962. To overcome the S.Mk 1's lack of power, the 84 Buccaneer S.Mk 2s were powered by the 5,105-kg (11,200-lb) thrust Rolls-Royce Spey Mk 101 turbofan, and with this engine displayed an all-round improvement in performance. The Royal Navy received its first aircraft in October 1965. The type had greater range than the S.Mk 1, but was also equipped for inflight refuelling. The similar Buccaneer S.Mk 50 was procured by South Africa, this model also having a 3,629-kg (8,000-lb) thrust Bristol Siddeley Stentor rocket motor for improved 'hot and high' take-off.

With the demise of the Navy's large carriers, some 70 S.Mk 2s were reallocated to the RAF from 1969 Buccaneer S.Mk 2As. Updated aircraft with provision for the Martel ASM became Buccaneer S.Mk 2Bs, and another 43 new aircraft were ordered to this standard. Further upgrades were made to RAF aircraft to extend their service career.

Buccaneer S.Mk 2B

BLACKBURN BUCCANEER S.Mk 2
Role: Low-level strike
Crew/Accommodation: Two
Power Plant: Two 5,035 kgp (11,100 lb s.t.) Rolls-Royce Spey Mk 101 turbofans
Dimensions: Span 13.41 m (44 ft); length 19.33 m (63.42 ft); wing area 47.82 m² (514.7 sq ft)
Weights: Empty 13,517 kg (29,800 lb); MTOW 28,123 kg (62,000 lb)
Performance: Maximum speed 1,040 km/h (561 knots) Mach 0.85 at 76 m (250 ft); operational ceiling 12,192 m (40,000+ ft); radius 1,738 km (938 naut. miles) with full warload
Load: Up to 3,175 kg (7,000 lb) of ordnance, including up to 1,815 kg (4,000 lb) internally, the remainder, typically Martel or Sea Eagle anti-ship missiles, being carried externally under the wings

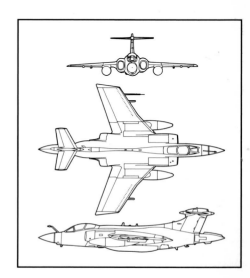

Buccaneer S.Mk 2B

DASSAULT ETENDARD Family (France)

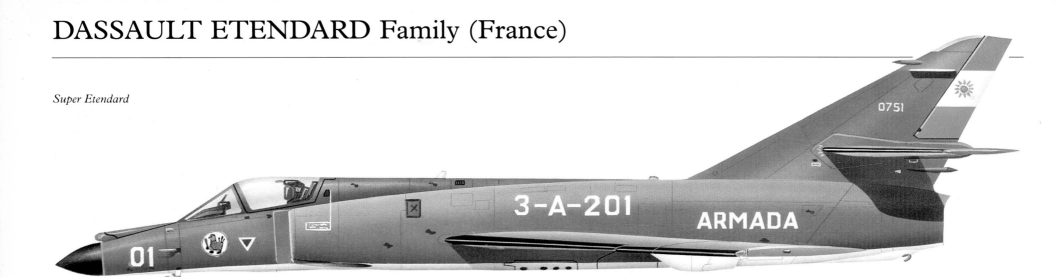

Super Etendard

By the middle of the 1950s the growing complexity of modern warplanes was beginning to dictate types of such size, weight, cost and lengthy gestation that considerable thought was given to lightweight attack fighters that could be developed comparatively quickly and cheaply for use on small airfields or even semi-prepared airstrips that would remove the need to build the large and costly air bases that were becoming increasingly vulnerable.

NATO formulated the requirement, and one of several contenders was the Etendard (Standard). Three prototypes were built, one of them with company funding, and the first of these flew in July 1956 as the Etendard II with two 1,100-kg (2,425-lb) thrust Turboméca Gabizo turbojets; the second prototypes had the 2,200-kg (4,850-lb) thrust Bristol Siddeley Orpheus BOr. 3 turbojet. The competition was won by the Fiat G91, but the company's own Etendard IV prototype, the Etendard IVM, larger than its half-brothers and designed to accommodate more

powerful engines, first flew in July 1956 and soon attracted naval interest as a carrierborne attack fighter.

One prototype and six pre-production aircraft validated revisions such as folding wingtips, naval equipment, a large rudder, beefed-up landing gear, and the 4,400-kg (9,700-lb) thrust SNECMA Atar 8B turbojet. Production totalled 90 aircraft, including 21 of the Etendard IVP reconnaissance/tanker variant. From 1970 Dassault revised the basic type as the Super Etendard, and the

first of two prototype conversions flew in October 1974. This model was given aerodynamic and structural revisions for transonic performance, and a modern nav/attack system including Agave multi-role radar for targeting of the AM.39 Exocet anti-ship missile. Seventy Super Etendards were delivered to the French navy from 1978, plus 12 to Argentina, with many French aircraft being modified to have the ability to carry ASMP nuclear stand-off missiles.

DASSAULT SUPER ETENDARD
Role: Carrierborne strike fighter
Crew/Accommodation: One
Power Plant: One 5,000-kgp (11,023-lb s.t.) SNECMA Atar 8K50 turbojet with reheat
Dimensions: Span 9.60 m (31.50 ft); length 14.31 m (46.90 ft); wing area 28.40 m² (307.00 sq ft)
Weights: Empty 6,300 kg (14,330 lb); MTOW 12,000 kg (26,455 lb)
Performance: Maximum speed 1,200 km/h (746 mph) at sea level; operational ceiling 13,700 m (45,000 ft); radius of action 880 km (547 miles) with one Exocet
Load: Two 30-mm cannon, plus up to 2,087 kg (4,600 lb) of externally carried weapons/missiles/fuel

Dassault Super Etendard

Dassault Super Etendard strike fighter

Dassault Super Etendards with two Etendard IVPs nearest the camera (Dassault)

GRUMMAN A-6 INTRUDER (U.S.A.)

A-6E Intruder

After the Korean War, the U.S. Navy wanted a jet-powered attacker able to undertake the pinpoint delivery of large warloads over long ranges and under all weather conditions. The resulting specification attracted 11 design submissions from eight companies, and at the very end of 1957 the G-128 design was selected for development as the A2F. Eight

YA2F-1 development aircraft were ordered, and the first of these flew in April 1960 with two 3,856-kg (8,500-lb) thrust Pratt & Whitney J52-P-6 turbojets. In 1962 the type was designated A-6, and in February 1963 the first of 482 A-6A production aircraft were delivered with 4,218-kg (9,300-lb) thrust J52-P-8A/B engines, a larger rudder, and the world's first digital nav/attack system. The Intruder had high maintenance requirements, but proved itself a superb attack platform during the Vietnam War.

The next three models were conversions, and comprised 19 A-6B day interdictors with simplified avionics and capability for the AGM-78 Standard anti-radar missile, 12 A-6C night attack aircraft with forward-looking infra-red and low-light-level TV sensors in an underfuselage turret, and 58 KA-6D 'buddy' refuelling tankers with a hose and drogue unit in the rear fuselage. This paved the way for the definitive A-6E attack model with J52-P-8B or -408 engines and

an improved nav/attack system based on solid-state electronics for greater reliability and reduced servicing requirements. Large numbers of A-6As were converted to this standard, with 205 A-6Es and A-6E/TRAM also newly built before all production ended in February 1992; TRAM aircraft featured the Target Recognition and Attack Multisensor package in a small undernose turret. The Intruder has now been withdrawn from service.

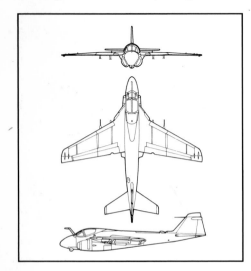

Grumman A-6E/TRAM Intruder

GRUMMAN A-6E/TRAM INTRUDER
Role: Naval carrierborne all-weather heavy strike (bomber)
Crew/Accommodation: Two
Power Plant: Two 4,218-kgp (9,300-lb s.t.) Pratt & Whitney J52-P-8B turbojets
Dimensions: Span 16.15 m (53 ft); length 16.69 m (54.75 ft); wing area 49.15 m² (529 sq ft)
Weights: Empty 12,525 kg (27,613 lb); MTOW 26,580 kg (58,600 lb) for carrier use
Performance: Maximum speed 1,036 km/h (644 mph) Mach 0.85 at sea level; operational ceiling 13,600 m (44,600 ft); range 1,738 km (1,080 miles) with full load
Load: Up to 8,165 kg (18,000 lb) of weapons – all externally carried

A Grumman A-6A Intruder

BRITISH AIRCRAFT CORPORATION TSR-2 (United Kingdom)

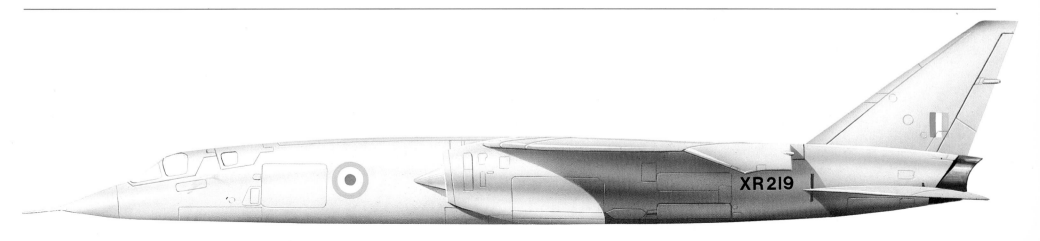

This is one of history's great 'aircraft that might have been'. The TSR-2 resulted from attempts, started as early as the 1950s, to produce a successor to the English Electric Canberra for long-range interdiction and reconnaissance. There were considerable difficulties in defining the type of aircraft required, and in envisaging the appropriate technology. Eventually it was announced in 1959 that the concept offered by the partnership of English Electric and Vickers-Armstrong was

to be developed as the TSR-2 weapons system providing the capability for supersonic penetration of enemy airspace at very low level for the accurate delivery of conventional and/or nuclear weapons. In configuration the TSR-2 was a high-wing monoplane with tandem seating for the crew of two, highly swept wings with downturned tips and wide-span blown trailing-edge flaps to provide STOL performance, and a swept tail unit, the surfaces of which provided

control in all three planes. The onboard electronic suite included an air-data system, inertial navigation system, forward-looking radar, and side-looking radar the data of which were integrated via an advanced computer to provide terrain-following capability and, on the pilot's head-up display and navigator's head-down displays, navigation cues and information relevant to weapon arming and release.

The result was an advanced but potentially formidable warplane that first flew in September 1964. As was

only to be expected in so complex a machine, there were a number of problems. These were in the process of being solved when rising costs and political antipathy persuaded the Labour government to cancel the project in April 1965. Only the first of four completed aircraft had flown, and this had accumulated only 13 hours 14 minutes of flying time during 24 flights.

British Aircraft Corporation TSR-2

BRITISH AIRCRAFT CORPORATION TSR-2
Role: Long range, low-level strike and reconnaissance
Crew/Accommodation: Two
Power Plant: Two 13,800 kgp (30,600 lb s.t) Bristol-Siddeley Olympus B.01.22R turbojets with reheat
Dimensions: Span 11.32 m (37.14 ft) length 27.14 m (89.04 ft); wing area 65.30 m² (702.90 sq ft)
Weights: Empty 24,834 kg (54,750 lb) MTOW 46,357 kg (102,200 lb)
Performance: Maximum speed 1,344+ km/h (725+ knots) Mach 1.1+ at sea level; operational ceiling 17,374+ m (57,000+ ft); radius 1,853 km (1,000 naut. miles)
Load: Up to 4,536 kg (10,000 lb) of weaponry/ fuel

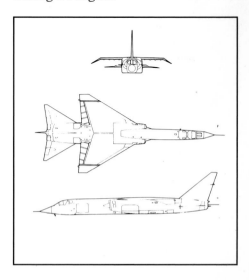

British Aircraft Corporation TSR-2

Dassault Mirage IVPs taking fuel from a C-135FR tanker (SIRPA 'AIR')

DASSAULT MIRAGE IV (FRANCE)

Mirage IVA

Requiring a supersonic delivery platform for the atomic bomb that was then the French nuclear deterrent weapon, the French air force in 1954 issued a requirement for a bomber offering long-range as well as high speed. Dassault headed a consortium that looked first at the development of the Sud-Ouest S.O. 4050 Vautour but from 1956 turned its attentions to the potential of an earlier aborted Dassault twin-engined night fighter design. This resulted in the design of the Mirage

IV of what was in essence a scaled-up Mirage III with two engines and provision for a 60-kiloton AN22 free-fall bomb semi-recessed under the fuselage.

The prototype first flew in June 1959 on the power of two 6,000-kg (13,228-lb) thrust SNECMA Atar 9 turbojets, and soon demonstrated its ability to maintain Mach 2 speed at high altitude. There followed three pre-production aircraft with slightly larger overall dimensions and two 6,400-kg (14,110-lb) thrust Atar 9C

turbojets. The first of these flew in October 1961, and was more representative of the Mirage IVA production model with a circular radome under the fuselage for the antenna of the bombing radar. The last of these three aircraft was fully representative in its Atar 9K engines, inflight refuelling probe and definitive nav/attack system. Mirage IVA production totalled 62 aircraft. Twelve aircraft were later converted as Mirage IVR strategic reconnaissance platforms with the CT52 mission package in the erstwhile bomb station, and from 1983 another 18 aircraft were converted as Mirage IVP missile

carriers (plus one more later because of attrition loss). These were given a new nav/attack system and upgraded electronic defences, and were designed for low-level penetration of enemy airspace as the launchers for the ASMP nuclear-tipped stand-off missile. The strategic/tactical bomber role was finally ended in 1996, leaving only a single squadron of reconnaissance aircraft.

The fourth Dassault Mirage IVA prototype

DASSAULT MIRAGE IVA
Role: Supersonic strategic bomber
Crew/Accommodation: Two
Power Plant: Two 7,000 kgp (15,432 lb s.t.) SNECMA Atar 09K turbojets with reheat
Dimensions: Span 11.85 m (38.88 ft); length 23.50 m (77.08 ft); wing area 78.00 m² (839.58 sq ft)
Weights: Empty 14,500 kg (31,965 lb); MTOW 31,600 kg (69,665 lb)
Performance: Maximum speed 2,124 km/h (1,146 knots) Mach 2.2 at 11,000 m (36,088 ft); operational ceiling 20,000 m (65,616 ft); radius 1,600+ km (994+ miles) unrefuelled
Load: One megaton range nuclear bomb carried semi-recessed beneath fuselage

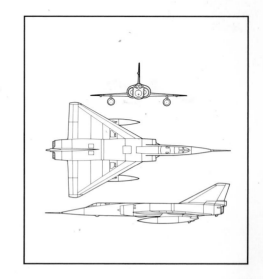

Dassault Mirage IVA

GENERAL DYNAMICS F-111 'Aardvark' (U.S.A.)

EF-111A Raven

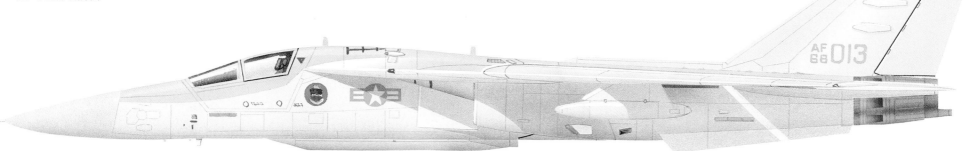

The F-111 was the world's first operational 'swing-wing' aircraft and remained in service as the U.S. Air Force's most potent all-weather long-range interdiction platform until July 1997, when it was belatedly named Aardvark. However, it remained operational with the Australian Air Force. The type originated from a 1960 requirement for a strike platform with the variable-geometry wings, the positions of which at minimum sweep would provide semi-STOL field performance at very high weights, at intermediate sweep long cruising range at high subsonic speed, and at maximum sweep very high dash performance. So versatile a tactical warplane suggested to the Department of Defense's civilian leadership the economic advantages of cheaper development and production costs if this land-based type could also be used as a basis for a new fleet defence fighter. Despite technical objections, the Tactical Fighter Experimental requirement was drawn up and orders placed for 23 pre-production aircraft (18 F-111As and five F-111Bs). The first of these flew in December 1964, but weight and performance problems led to the July 1968 cancellation of the F111B. The F111A also had problems before and after its March 1968 operational service debut in Vietnam, but despite an indifferent powerplant it matured into an exceptional combat aircraft. The most important tactical models were 158 F-111As with 8,391-kg (18,500-lb) thrust TF30-P-3 engines, 24 F-111Cs for Australia with the FB-111A's longer-span wings, 96 F-111Ds with 8,890-kg (19,600-lb) thrust TF30-P-9s, 94 F-111Es with 8,890-kg (19,600-lb) thrust TF30-P-103s, and 106 F-111Fs with 11,385-kg (25,100-lb) thrust TF30-P-111s and improved electronics; 42 of the F-111As were modified into EF-111A Raven electronic platforms for service from 1981; Ravens were retired in 1998. There is also a strategic model in the form of 76 FB-111As with wings of 2.13 m (7 ft 0 in) greater span, two extra wing hardpoints, 9,185-kg (20,150-lb) thrust TF30-P-7 engines, and revised electronics; many of these were later converted into F-111G tactical aircraft for use in the European theatre by the USAF as conventionally armed aircraft (now retired), with some also going to the RAAF.

General Dynamics F-111

GENERAL DYNAMICS F-111F
Role: Long-range, low-level variable-geometry strike
Crew/Accommodation: Two
Power Plant: Two 11,385-kgp (25,100-lb s.t.) Pratt & Whitney TF30-P-111 turbofans with reheat
Dimensions: Span 19.2 m (63.00 ft), swept 9.73 m (31.95 ft); length 22.4 m (73.5 ft); wing area 48.77 m² (525 sq ft)
Weights: Empty 21,700 kg (47,840 lb); MTOW 45,360 kg (100,000 lb)
Performance: Maximum speed Mach 2.5 at altitude or 1,471 km/h (914 mph) Mach 1.2 at sea level; operational ceiling 17,650 m (57,900 ft); range over 4,667 km (2,900 miles)
Load: One 22-mm multi-barrel cannon, plus up to 11,340 kg (25,000 lb) of ordnance/fuel

A General Dynamics F-111 in flight with its wings extended

VOUGHT A-7 CORSAIR II (U.S.A.)

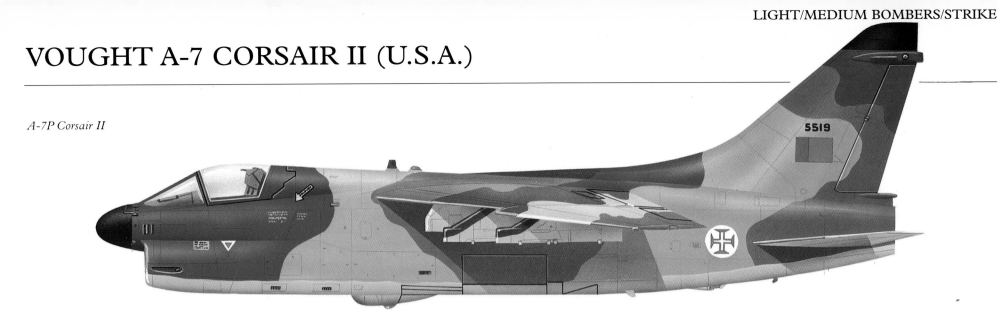

A-7P Corsair II

The A-7 was developed with great speed on the aerodynamic basis of the F-8 Crusader to provide the U.S. Navy with a medium-weight replacement for the light-weight Douglas A-4 Skyhawk in the carrierborne attack role, and in March 1964 the navy ordered three YA-7A prototypes. The first of these flew in September 1965 with the 5148-kg (11,350-lb) thrust Pratt & Whitney TF30-P-6 non-afterburning turbofan, and the flight test programme moved ahead with great speed. This allowed the Corsair II to enter service during February 1967 in the form of the A-7A with the same engine as the YA-7A. Production totalled 199 aircraft of this initial model, and was followed by 196 examples of the A-7B with the 5534-kg (12,200-lb) thrust TF30-P-8 that was later upgraded to -408

standard, and by 67 examples of the A-7C with the 6078-kg (13,400-lb) thrust TF309-P-408 and the armament/avionics suite of the later A-7E variant.

In December 1965 the U.S. Air Force decided to adopt a version with a different engine, the Rolls-Royce Spey turbofan in its licence-built form as the Allison TF41. The USAF series was now named Corsair II, and the first model was the A-7D, of which 459 were built with the 6577-kg (14,500-lb) thrust TF41-A-1, a 20-mm six-barrel rotary cannon in place of the Corsair II's two 20-mm single-barrel cannon, a much improved nav/attack package and, as a retrofit,

manoeuvring flaps and the 'Pave Penny' laser tracker. This model was mirrored by the Navy's A-7E, of which 551 were built with the 6804-kg (15,000-lb) thrust TF41-A-2 and, as a retrofit, a forward-looking infra-red sensor. There have been some two-seat versions and limited exports, but nothing came of the A-7 Plus radical development that was evaluated as the YA-7F with advanced electronics and the combination of more power and a revised airframe for supersonic performance.

A Vought A-7E Corsair II

VOUGHT A-7E CORSAIR II
Role: Naval carrierborne strike
Crew/Accommodation: One
Power Plant: One 6,804 kgp (15,000 lb s.t.) Allison/Rolls-Royce TF41-A-1 turbofan
Dimensions: Span 11.8 m (38.75 ft); length 14.06 m (46.13 ft); wing area 34.83 m² (375 sq ft)
Weights: Empty 8,592 kg (18,942 lb); MTOW 19,051 kg (42,000 lb)
Performance: Maximum speed 1,060 km/h (572 knots) at sea level; operational ceiling 13,106 m (43,000 ft); range 908 km (489 naut. miles) with 2,722 kg (6,000 lb) bombload
Load: One 6-barrel 20 mm cannon, plus up to 6,804 kg (15,000 lb) of weapons

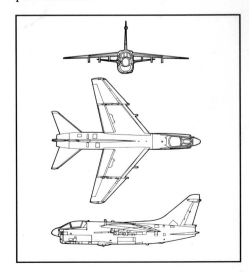

Vought A-7E Corsair II

BRITISH AEROSPACE HARRIER Family (United Kingdom)

Harrier GR.Mk 3

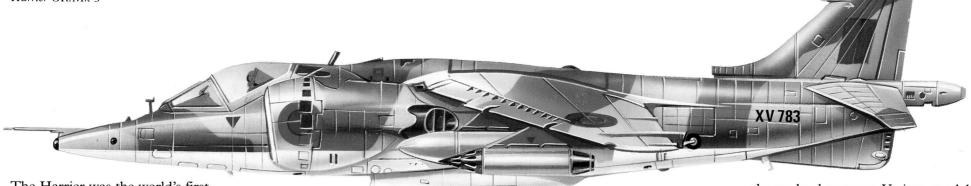

The Harrier was the world's first operational VTOL combat aircraft, and at its core is the remarkable Rolls-Royce (Bristol Siddeley) Pegasus vectored-thrust turbofan. The type was pioneered in the form of six P. 1127 prototypes. The first of these made its initial hovering flights, in tethered mode, during October 1960, and the first transition flights between direct-thrust hovering and wingborne forward flight followed during September 1961. Such was the potential of this experimental type that nine Kestrel F(GA).Mk 1

evaluation aircraft were built for a combined British, U.S. and West German trials squadron.

The Harrier became the operational version, and the main types were the Harrier GR.Mk 1 with the 8,618-kg (19,000-lb) thrust Pegasus Mk 101, the GR.Mk 1A with the 9,072-kg (20,000-lb) thrust Pegasus Mk 102, and the GR.Mk 3 with the 9,752-kg (21,000-lb) thrust Pegasus Mk 103 and revised nose accommodating a laser ranger and marked-target seeker. Combat-capable two-seat trainers were also

built. The U.S. Marine Corps used the Harrier as the AV-8A single-seater (of which many were upgraded to AV-8C standard) and TAV-8A two-seater examples were exported to Spain with the local name Matador.

A much improved variant of Harrier was developed by McDonnell Douglas and BAe as the Harrier II, first flown in 1981 and featuring a larger wing of composite construction with leading-edge root extensions, other aerodynamic improvements, better avionics and more engine power, allowing twice

the payload or range. Various models of the Pegasus 11 engine have been fitted, the most powerful being the 10,795-kg (23,800-lb) thrust Pegasus 11-61 in late U.S. Marine Corps aircraft (designated F402-RR-408A), as also used in Spanish Matador IIs and Italian trainers.

U.S. Marine Corps Harrier IIs are designated AV-8B, while the current RAF version is the GR.Mk 7, upgraded from GR. Mk 5/5As to permit night attack. The companies have also developed the Harrier II Plus with APG-65 radar for expanded roles. Naval versions of Harrier became Sea Harrier, now in its latest F/A Mk 2 form for the Royal Navy.

Harrier GR.Mk 3

BRITISH AEROSPACE HARRIER GR. Mk 7
Role: Close air support and interdiction
Crew/Accommodation: One
Power Plant: One 9,775-kgp (21,550-lb s.t.) Rolls-Royce Pegasus 11 Mk 105 vectored-thrust turbofan
Dimensions: Span 9.25 m (30.33 ft); length 14.53 m (47.66 ft); wing area 21.37 m² (230 sq ft)
Weights: Empty 6,831–7,123 kg (15,060–15,705 lb); MTOW 14,515 kg (32,000 lb)
Performance: Maximum speed Mach 0.98; radius of action 1,111 km (691 miles) with two 1,000-lb bombs, three BL 755s and two drop tanks
Load: Two 25-mm externally mounted cannon, plus up to 4,900 kg (10,800 lb) of ordnance/fuel

Harrier GR.Mk 7

SEPECAT JAGUAR (France/United Kingdom)

Jaguar GR.Mk 1A

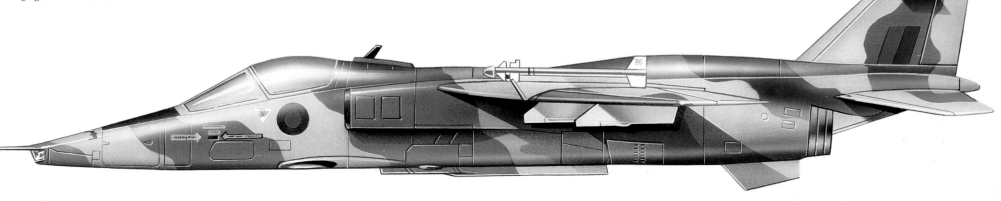

In the early 1960s, the British and French air forces each showed interest in a dual-role supersonic warplane able to function as a tandem-seat operational trainer and single-seat attack aircraft. The similarity of the two requirements suggested a collaborative design, development and production programme, and in May 1965 the British and French governments signed an agreement for such a programme. Several British and French designs were studied before the Breguet Br.121 concept was selected as the basis for the new warplane, the development of which was undertaken by the Société Européenne de Production de l'Avion Ecole de Combat at d'Appui Tactique (SEPECAT) formed by the British Aircraft Corporation and Breguet. An equivalent engine grouping combined Rolls-Royce and Turboméca for the selected Adour afterburning turbofan.

The Jaguar first flew in September 1968 as a conventional monoplane with swept flying surfaces and retractable tricycle landing gear, a shoulder-set wing being selected as this provided good ground clearance for the wide assortment of disposable stores carried on four underwing hardpoints in addition to a centreline hardpoint under the fuselage.

Such were the capabilities of the aircraft that major production was initiated, with variants as the Jaguar A and S single-seat attack aircraft (160 and 165 aircraft respectively for the French and British air forces, of which the latter has considerably upgraded its aircraft with greater power and a more advanced nav/attack system, and in GR. Mk 3 form) plus Jaguar E and Jaguar B trainers (40 and 38 aircraft respectively for the French and British air forces). There has also been the Jaguar International for the export market, with overwing hardpoints for air-to-air missiles as standard, uprated engines and, in Indian aircraft, an improved nav/attack system including radar in some aircraft. Customers were Ecuador, Nigeria, Oman and India, plus others built in India by HAL as Shamshers (Indian total of 131 aircraft).

A SEPECAT Jaguar GR.Mk 1 of the RAF's No. 6 Squadron

SEPECAT JAGUAR INTERNATIONAL
Role: Low-level strike fighter and maritime strike
Crew/Accommodation: One
Power Plant: Two 3,811-kgp (8,400-lb s.t.) Rolls-Royce/Turboméca Adour Mk 811 turbofans with reheat
Dimensions: Span 8.69 m (28.5 ft); length 15.52 m (50.92 ft) as single-seater, without probe; wing area 24 m² (258.33 sq ft)
Weights: Empty 7,000 kg (15,432 lb); MTOW 15,700 kg (34,613 lb)
Performance: Maximum speed 1,350 km/h (839 mph) Mach 1.1 at sea level; radius of action 852 km (529 miles) with 3,629 kg (8,000 lb) warload
Load: Two 30-mm cannon, plus up to 4,536 kg (10,000 lb) of weapons, including bombs, rockets or air-to-surface missiles, plus two short-range air-to-air missiles

SEPECAT Jaguar GR.Mk 1A

TUPOLEV Tu-22M 'BACKFIRE' (U.S.S.R.)

Tu-22M 'Backfire'

Known to NATO as the 'Backfire', the Tu-22M is the world's only modern medium bomber, and was conceived to make nuclear or conventional strikes against targets in Western Europe and China, plus attack aircraft carriers and other large ships in a maritime role. It was specified to require a 2,000 km/h dash speed and Mach 0.9 low-level penetration speed while armed with

AS-4 'Kitchen' missiles. It was to be a supersonic 'swing-wing' successor to the Tu-16 'Badger' via the interim supersonic Tu-22 'Blinder'.

The new bomber first flew in August 1969 and 'Backfire-A' pre-series aircraft appeared from 1971. Tu-22M2 'Backfire-B' initial large-scale production aircraft joined the Soviet air force from 1975, fitted with new avionics and two cannon

in the tail, but most importantly offering a range of 2,753 nautical miles and speed of 972 knots.

The Tu-22M3 'Backfire-C' entered service in 1983 and introduced uprated NK-25 engines, modified forward fuselage with larger wedge air inlets and other improvements, making it over twice as combat-capable as the Tu-22M2. Since 1992, M3s have been further

upgraded to M5s, with changes including those to the radar and missiles carried. Tu-22MP and Tu-22MR are electronic warfare and reconnaissance versions respectively.

Tu-22 operators are the Russian air force and navy plus Ukraine.

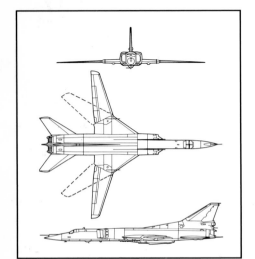

Tupolev Tu-22M 'Backfire-C'

TUPOLEV Tu-22M 'BACKFIRE-C'
Role: Bomber/reconnaissance with variable-geometry wing
Crew/Accommodation: Four
Power Plant: Two 25,000-kgp (55,115 s.t.) Samara NK-25 turbofans with reheat
Dimensions: Span 34.28 m (112.5 ft), swept 23.3 m (76.4 ft); length 42.46 m (139.33 ft); wing area 183.58 m² (1,976 sq ft)
Weights: MTOW 124,000 kg (273,373 lb) without JATO rockets
Performance: Maximum speed 2,000 km/h (1,243 mph) Mach 1.8 at high altitude; operational ceiling 14,000 m (45,925 ft); radius of action 2,200 km (1,367 miles) with one 'Kitchen' missile and unrefuelled
Load: two 23-mm cannon, plus 24,000 kg (52,910 lb) of weapons, including three AS-4 'Kitchen' missiles or a mix with AS-16 'Kick-back' short-range missiles on a rotary launcher, nuclear or conventional bombs, mines, etc.

Tupolev Tu-22M 'Backfire-B'

YAKOVLEV Yak-38 'FORGER' (U.S.S.R.)

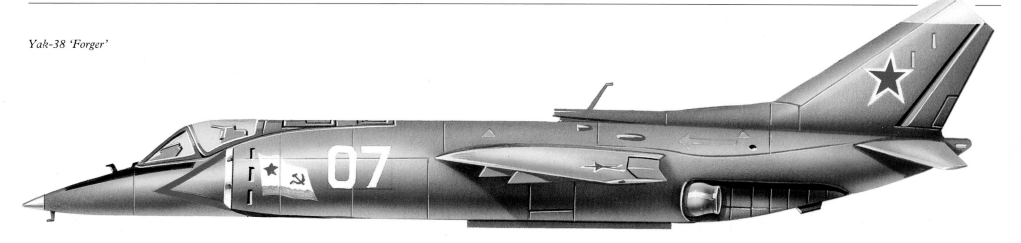

Yak-38 'Forger'

The Yak-38 (or Yak-36M for prototype) was the first-ever and so far only Soviet operational vertical take-off (VSTOL) combat aeroplane, of which 231 were built for the navy, but was withdrawn from service in the early 1990s. Supersonic replacements to be used as carrierborne interceptors, the Yakovlev Yak-41 and Yak-43 (the former known to NATO as

'Freestyle' and first flown in 1987) were subsequently abandoned before reaching service status.

The 'Forger' prototype first flew in January 1971, with the thrust-vectoring turbojet in the rear fuselage complemented by two small liftjets in the forward fuselage and mounted almost vertically to exhaust downward. A fully automatic control system was employed during take-off/landing, to ensure correct use of engines and jet reaction

nozzles/aerodynamic controls used in association with devices on board ship. Subsequently, short take-offs became more common than vertical, using similar methods of control.

The 'Forger-A' was a single-seat type designed principally to provide Soviet naval forces with experience in the operation of such aircraft. The type is therefore limited in terms of performance, warload and electronics, but still provided Soviet aircraft

carriers/cruiser carriers with useful interception and attack capabilities in areas too distant for the involvement of land-based air defences. The original production 'Forger-A' had less powerful liftjets than the improved Yak-38M 'Forger-A' of 1984 onwards service. The Yak-38UV was known to NATO as 'Forger-B' and was the tandem two-seat conversion trainer variant with the fuselage lengthened to accommodate the second cockpit.

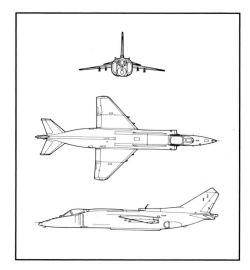

Yak-38 'Forger-A'

YAKOVLEV Yak-38M 'FORGER-A'
Role: Vertical take-off and landing naval strike fighter
Crew/Accommodation: One
Power Plant: One 6,700-kgp (14,770-lb s.t.) Soyuz R-28V-300 vectored-thrust turbojet plus two 3,250 kgp (7,165 lb s.t.) Rybinsk RD-36 lift turbojets
Dimensions: Span 7.3 m (24 ft); length 15.5 m (51 ft); wing area 18.5 m² (199 sq ft)
Weights: MTOW 11,700 kg (25,794 lb)
Performance: Maximum speed 1,164 km/h (723 mph) Mach 0.95 at sea level; operational ceiling 12,000 m (39,370 ft); radius of action 371 km (230 miles)
Load: Up to 2,000 kg (4,409 lb) of externally carried weapons, including two AA-8 'Aphid' air-to-air missiles

Yak-38 'Forger-As'

FAIRCHILD REPUBLIC A-10 THUNDERBOLT II (U.S.A.)

A-10A Thunderbolt II

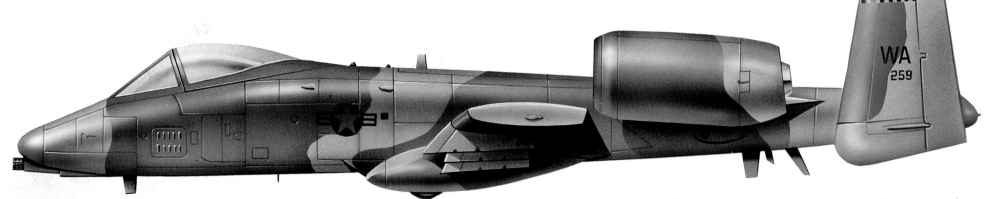

First flown in May 1972 as the YA-10A after Republic Aviation had become a division of Fairchild, the Thunderbolt II was developed to meet the U.S. Air Force's Attack Experimental requirement of 1967. The two YA-10A prototypes were competitively evaluated against the two YA-9s produced by Northrop, and the Fairchild Republic design was declared winner of the competition in January 1973. The requirement called for a specialist close-support and anti-tank aircraft offering high rates of survival from ground fire, a high-subsonic speed combined with good low-speed manoeuvrability, and a heavy weapon load.

The particular nature of its role dictated the Thunderbolt II's peculiar configuration with two turbofan engines located high on the fuselage sides between the wings and tailplane, and straight flying surfaces that restrict outright performance but enhance take-off performance and agility at very low level. To reduce the effect of anti-aircraft fire, all major systems are duplicated, extensive armour is carried, and vulnerable systems such as the engines are both duplicated and shielded as much as possible from ground detection and thus from ground fire. The first of 713 production aircraft were delivered in 1975, and though the type remains in valuable service in both A-10A attack and OA-10A lightly-armed forward air control variants, many have been passed to U.S. Air National Guard and Air Force Reserve units.

The core of the A-10A is the massive GAU-8/A Avenger seven-barrel cannon that occupies most of the forward fuselage and carries 1,174 rounds of 30-mm anti-tank ammunition delivering a pyrophoric penetrator of depleted uranium. A large load of other weapons, both 'smart' and 'dumb', can be carried on no fewer than 11 hardpoints.

A Fairchild Republic A-10A Thunderbolt II

FAIRCHILD REPUBLIC A-10A THUNDERBOLT II
Role: Close air support
Crew/Accommodation: One
Power Plant: Two 4,112-kgp (9,065-lb s.t.) General Electric TF34-GE-100 turbofans
Dimensions: Span 17.53 m (57.5 ft); length 16.25 m (53.33 ft); wing area 47.01m² (506 sq ft)
Weights: Empty 12,700 kg (28,000 lb); MTOW 23,586 kg (52,000 lb)
Performance: Maximum speed 707 km/h (439 mph) without external weapons; operational ceiling 10,575 m (34,700 ft); radius of action 763 km (474 miles)
Load: One 30-mm multi-barrel cannon, plus up to 7,250 kg (16,000 lb) of externally carried weapons

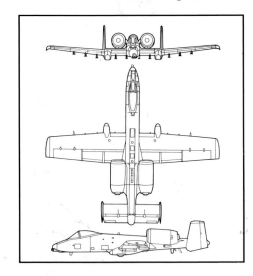

A-10A Thunderbolt II

PANAVIA TORNADO (Italy/United Kingdom/ West Germany)

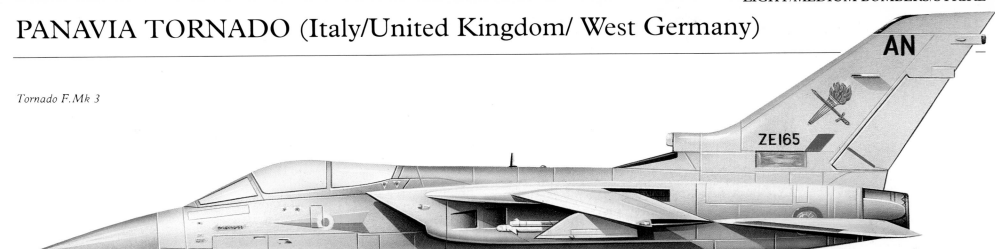

Tornado F.Mk 3

Currently one of the NATO alliance's premier front-line aircraft types, the Tornado was planned from the late 1960s as a multi-role combat aircraft able to operate from and into short or damaged runways for long-range interdiction missions at high speed and very low level. The keys to the mission are variable-geometry wings able to sweep from 25° spread to 67° fully swept and carrying an extensive array of high-lift devices on their leading edges and trailing edges,

advanced high by-pass turbofan engines that offer low fuel burn at cruise speed and high afterburning thrust, and an advanced sensor and electronic suite. This suite is based on a capable nav/attack system that includes attack and terrain-following radars, an inertial navigation system, and a triplex fly-by-wire control system.

The first of the Tornado prototypes flew in August 1974, and after a protracted development

the first production Tornados for the RAF and Luftwaffe were handed over in June 1979, followed eventually by the first for Italy (in 1981). The three main variants are the Tornado IDS baseline interdiction and strike warplane, the Tornado ADV air-defence fighter with different radar and weapons (including four semi-recessed Sky Flash air-to-air missiles) in a longer fuselage, and the Tornado ECR electronic combat and reconnaissance type. The British RAF version of the

IDS was delivered as the Tornado GR.Mk 1, while Tornado GR.Mk 1A became the reconnaissance derivative and GR.Mk IB a maritime attack model carrying two Sea Eagle missiles; GR.Mk 4/4As are current upgrades of Mk 1/1As. The air defence variant interceptor for the RAF is currently flown in F.Mk 3 version, while Italy is leasing 24 pending Eurofighter deliveries. Including exports of IDS/ADVs to Saudi Arabia, total Tornado production amounted to 781 IDS/ECRs and 194 ADVs.

Panavia Tornado IDSs of the German navy's Marinefliegergeschwader 1

PANAVIA TORNADO IDS
Role: All-weather, low-level strike and reconnaissance
Crew/Accommodation: Two
Power Plant: Two 7,257-kgp (16,000-lb s.t.) Turbo-Union RB199 Mk 103 turbofans with reheat
Dimensions: Span 13.9m (45.6 ft), swept 8.6 m (28.2 ft); length 16.7 m (54.8 ft); wing area 26.6 m² (286.3 sq ft)
Weights: Empty 14,000 kg (30,864 lb); MTOW 28,000 kg (61,729 lb)
Performance: Maximum speed Mach 2.2 clean or 1,483 km/h (921 mph), Mach 1.2 at 152 m (500 ft); operational ceiling 15,240+ m (50,000+ ft); radius of action typically 1,482 km (921 miles) with four 1,000-lb bombs, two Sidewinders and two drop tanks
Load: Two 27-mm cannon, plus up to 9,000 kg (19,842 lb) of externally carried weaponry and fuel

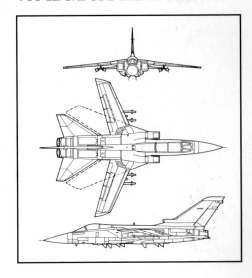

Panavia Tornado F.Mk 3

51

LOCKHEED MARTIN F-117 NIGHTHAWK (U.S.A.)

F-117A

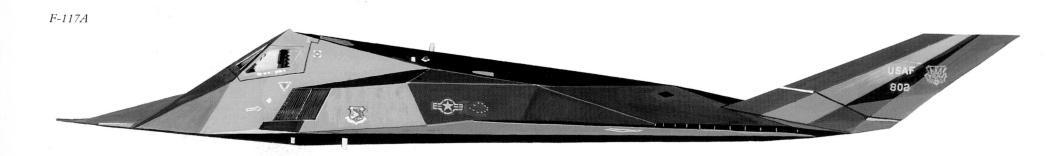

The world's first fully 'stealth' aircraft to reach operational status, the F-117 was developed to penetrate dense threat environments during the hours of darkness, and destroy critical or high-value enemy targets with amazing accuracy. Its strange shape and secret nature comes from its ability to counter radar, infra-red, visual, contrails, engine smoke, acoustic and electromagnetic signatures.

Development began with two small XST Have Blue technology demonstrators, the first flown in December 1977, and five FSD flight test aircraft (first flown in January 1981). Delivery of 59 F-117As to the USAF started in August 1982 and initial operational capability was achieved in October 1983. The public did not hear of the aircraft until 1988. Its first combat use came in December 1989 when two aircraft dropped laser-guided bombs on barracks in Panama during Operation Just Cause, while during the 1991 Gulf War 42 flew 1,271 missions.

The F-117A's airframe is of the 'lifting body' type, with the outer faceted skin formed from flat surfaces arranged at angles to overcome enemy radars. All aspects of the design were carefully considered, including the air intakes which have heated grids to block radar energy, while the engine nozzles are horizontal slots that produce a thin exhaust plume that is mixed with cold air and quickly dispersed. No radar is carried, the pilot instead relying on sophisticated navigation and attack systems, automated mission planning, and forward/downward-looking infra-red devices.

Lockheed Martin F-117A Nighthawk

LOCKHEED MARTIN F-117A
Role: Low-observability strike
Crew/Accommodation: One
Power Plant: Two 4,899-kgp (10,800-lb s.t.) General Electric F404-GE-F1D2 non-reheated turbofans
Dimensions: Span 13.20 m (43.44 ft); length 20.09 m (65.92 ft); wing area 84.82 m² (913 sq ft)
Weights: MTOW 23,814 kg (52,500 lb)
Performance: Maximum speed 1,040 km/h (646 mph); radius of action 1,111 km (691 miles) with full weapon load, unrefuelled
Load: Two laser-guided 2,000-lb bombs in the bay, or other weapons up to 2,268 kg (5,000 lb)

U.S.A.F. Lockheed Martin F-117A Nighthawk

USAF Lockheed Martin F-117A Nighthawk

Maritime Patrol

Few people fully appreciate the importance of maritime aircraft in the annals of aviation. Two years before the Wright brothers flew for the first time in their powered *Flyer*, Austrian Wilhelm Kress 'hopped' his tandem-wing powered seaplane from the Tullnerbach reservoir (in 1901), experiments which preceded even the famous Potomac River trials by American Samuel Pierpoint Langley.

Maritime aircraft were widely used during World War I, both in floatplane form and as flying-boats. The German navy made particular use of floatplanes as naval station defence fighters and for reconnaissance patrol and fighter escort, while Claude Dornier became responsible for several giant flying-boats from 1915 that were produced as Zeppelin-Lindau Rs type prototypes under the patronage of Count von Zeppelin of airship fame. Although these Dornier-designed aircraft were not significant to the German war effort, it gave the young designer the means to go on and conceive some of the finest flying-boats of the inter-war period.

Other fighting nations also produced maritime aircraft, not least the truly beautifully-styled small Italian Macchi flying-boat fighters and maritime patrol aircraft that were operational from 1917. Overall, though, it was Britain that led the world in the development and use of large flying-boats, aircraft which performed brilliantly in combatting both German U-boat submarines and Zeppelin airships. Interestingly, the best of these was without question the R.N.A.S.'s Felixstowe F.2A/F.3, developed by Sqdn. Cdr. John C. Porte from the earlier and less successful American Curtiss H.12 Large America which could trace its ancestry to an original pre-war flying-boat intended to attempt a transatlantic flight. Despite its bulk and weight, the Felixstowe had the added virtue of being highly manoeuvrable, and on 4 June 1918 this was put to the test when three F.2As defended a fourth aircraft (which had alighted due to a fuel blockage) from 14 attacking enemy seaplanes, shooting down six in the process. Indeed, as testimony to the Felixstowe design, Curtiss went on to produce a version as the F-5L for the U.S. Navy, as an American-built example of a British-improved flying-boat of Curtiss original design!

Flying-boats were ideally suited to long over-water flights, and post-war were highly developed for both military and commercial use. They remained much prized during World War II for an expanded number of roles, including spotter-reconnaissance and air-sea rescue, the latter often by small craft launched from ships at sea as well as from land and coastal waters. But it was the large flying-boats that made such an impact on anti-submarine warfare and convoy escort. The RAF Short Sunderland, for example, proved so successful that the final aircraft were not retired by the RAF until 1959, having first become operational in 1938, while the American Consolidated PBY Catalina was used from 1941 in a whole gamut of roles and became the most-produced flying-boat of all time.

Germany, as others, built fine flying-boats, among the best remembered being the unorthodox Blohm und Voss Bv 138 for reconnaissance and some giant types from the same company. The sleek Dornier Do 24, despite its capability to carry bombs, is thought never to have been employed on any offensive mission. Instead, Germany placed its faith partly in the Focke-Wulf Fw 200 Condor landplane for long-range maritime reconnaissance and maritime bomber duties, as one of the few German four-engined bombers of that war. This proved extremely successful in its combined operations with German U-boats against Allied convoys, until confronted by fighters from new escort carriers or catapult-launched from merchant ships. It may be said, therefore, that Condor led the way to post-war preferences towards landplanes and, since the 1950s, most of the world's purpose-built maritime patrol aircraft have been of landplane design.

Picture: The Dassault Atlantique 2 has been developed from the original Atlantic of 1961 first appearance, which was originally conceived to offer NATO forces a standardized long-range maritime patrol and anti-submarine landplane. Atlantic was the first European landplane specifically designed for anti-submarine and anti-surface vessel use

CONSOLIDATED PBY CATALINA (U.S.A.)

PBY-1 Catalina

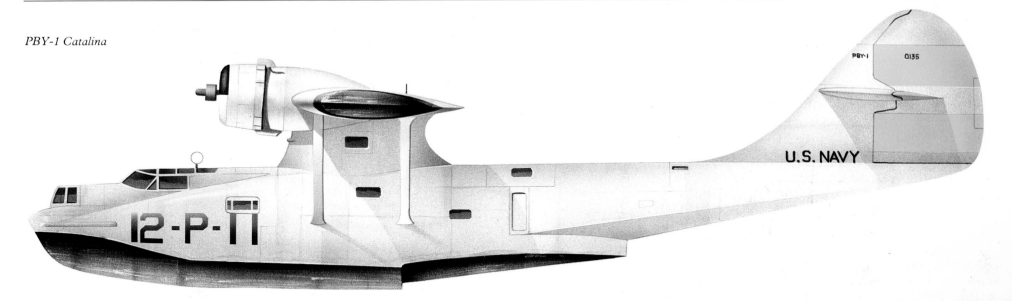

In the early 1930s, the U.S. Navy issued a requirement for a patrol flying boat that offered greater range and payload than the Consolidated P2Y and Martin P3M then in service. Design proposals were received from Consolidated and Douglas, and single prototypes of each were ordered. The Douglas

type was restricted to a single XP3D-1 prototype, but the Consolidated Model 28 became one of the most important flying-boats ever developed. The XP3Y-1 prototype first flew in March 1935 and was a large machine with a wide two-step hull, a strut-braced parasol wing mounted on top of a massive pylon that accommodated the flight engineer, and stabilizing

floats that retracted in flight to become the wingtips and so reduce drag.

The type clearly possessed considerable potential and after being reworked as a patrol bomber was ordered into production as the PBY-1, of which 60 were built with 671-kW (900-hp) R-1830-64 radial engines. The following PBY-2 had equipment improvements, and production totalled 50. Next came 66 PBY-3s with 746-kW (1,000-hp) R-1830-66 engines and 33 PBY-4s with 783-kW (1,050-hp) R-1830-72 engines. The generally improved PBY-5 with 895-kW (1,200-lb) R-1830-82 or -92 engines was the definitive flying-boat model and many hundreds were built, complemented by many PYB-5A and 5B amphibians, including those for lend-lease to Britain. The Naval Aircraft Factory produced 156 of a PBN-1 Nomad version of the PBY-5 with aerodynamic and hydrodynamic improvements, and 235 of a comparable amphibian model were built by Consolidated

as the PBY-6A for the U.S. Navy, USAAF and Russia, making 2,398 Catalinas built by Consolidated. The basic type was also produced in Canada by Canadian Vickers and Boeing, plus in the U.S.S.R. as the GST, while the U.K. adopted the aircraft in several variants with the name Catalina that has since been generally adopted for all PBY models.

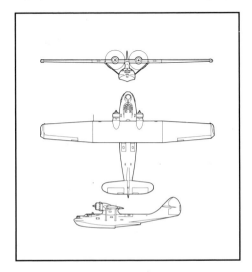

Consolidated PBY Catalina

CONSOLIDATED PBY-5 (RAF CATALINA Mk IV)

Role: Long-range maritime patrol bomber flying boat

Crew/Accommodation: Nine

Power Plant: Two, 1,200 hp Pratt & Whitney R-1830-92 Twin Wasp air-cooled radials

Dimensions: Span 37.10 m (104 ft); length 19.47 m (63.88 ft); wing area 130.1 m² (1,400 sq ft)

Weights: Empty 7,809 kg (17,200 lb); MTOW 15,436 kg (34,000 lb)

Performance: Cruise speed 182 km/h (113 mph) at sea level; operational ceiling 5,517 m (18,100 ft); range 4,812 km (2,990 miles) with full warload

Load: Two .5 inch and two .303 inch machine guns, plus up to 1,816 kg (4,000 lb) of torpedoes, depth charges or bombs carried externally

The Consolidated PBY-6A Catalina

SHORT SUNDERLAND Family (United Kingdom)

Sunderland Mk I

L2163

The Sunderland was the U.K.'s premier maritime reconnaissance flying boat of World War II, and derived ultimately from the S.23 class of civil 'Empire' flying boats. The prototype flew in October 1937 with 753-kW (1,010-hp) Bristol Pegasus XXII radials, and was the first British flying boat to have power-operated defensive gun turrets. The prototype proved most satisfactory, and production of this variant totalled 90

before it was overtaken on the lines by the Sunderland Mk II with 794-kW (1,065-hp) Pegasus XVIII radials and a power-operated dorsal turret in place of the Mk I's two 7.7-mm (0.303-in) beam guns in manually operated waist positions.

These 43 'boats were in turn succeeded by the Sunderland Mk III, which was the most extensively built variant with 456 being built. This variant had a hull revised with a faired step, and some 'boats were to the Sunderland Mk IIIA standard with ASV. Mk III surface-search radar. The Sunderland Mk IV was developed for Pacific operations and became the S.45 Seaford, of which a mere 10 examples (three prototypes and seven production 'boats) were built with 1253- and 1283-kW (1,680- and 1,720-hp) Bristol Hercules XVII and XIX radials respectively. The last Sunderland variant was the Mk V, of which 150 were built with 895-kW

(1,200-hp) Pratt & Whitney R-1830-90B radials and ASV. Mk VIC radar under the wingtips; the more powerful engines allowed the type to operate at cruising rather than maximum engine revolutions, which improved engine life and aided economical running.

Sunderlands were also used for civil transport, the first of 24 Sunderland

Mk IIIs being handed over to British Airways in March 1943. The 'boats were later brought up to more comfortable standard as Hythes, and were then revised as Sandringham with R-1830-92 radials and, in addition, neat aerodynamic fairings over the erstwhile nose and tail turret positions.

SHORT SUNDERLAND Mk V
Role: Anti-submarine/maritime patrol
Crew/Accommodation: Seven
Power Plant: Four 1,200 hp Pratt & Whitney R-1830-90B Twin Wasp air-cooled radials
Dimensions: Span 34.39 m (112.77 ft); length 26 m (85.33 ft); wing area 156.6 m² (1,687 sq ft)
Weights: Empty 16,783 kg (37,000 lb); MTOW 27,250 kg (60,000 lb)
Performance: Maximum speed 343 km/h (213 mph) at 1,525 m (5,000 ft); operational ceiling 5,455 m (17,900 ft); range 4,300 km (2,690 miles) with maximum fuel
Load: Six .5 inch machine guns and eight .303 inch machine guns, plus up to 908 kg (2,000 lb) of bombs/depth charges

Sunderland Mk II

Sunderland Mk V

ARADO Ar 196 (Germany)

Ar 196A-3

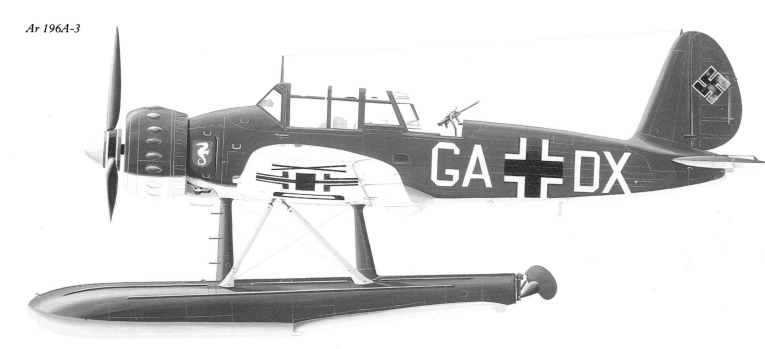

contender from the running and, after testing of the two alighting gear arrangements, the Arado type was ordered into production as the Ar 196A with twin floats. Total construction was 546 aircraft, including machines built in Dutch and French factories under German control.

The type was built in two main streams for shipboard and coastal use. The shipboard stream comprised 20 Ar 196A-1s with two wing-mounted 7.92-mm (0.312-in) machine guns and 24 strengthened Ar 196A-4s based on the Ar 196A-3. The coastal stream comprised 391 examples of the Ar 196A-2 with two 20-mm wing-mounted cannon and the strengthened Ar 196A-3 with a variable-pitch propeller, and 69 examples of the Ar 196A-5 with better radio and a twin rather than single machine-gun installation for the radio-operator/gunner. The Ar 196 was used in most of the German theatres during World War II.

The Ar 196 was designed to meet a 1936 requirement for a floatplane reconnaissance aircraft to succeed the same company's Ar 95 biplane, and was intended for catapult-launched use from German major surface warships, though a secondary coastal patrol capability was also envisaged. The type clearly had more than a passing kinship with the Ar 95, but was an all-metal monoplane and was designed for use on either twin floats or a combination of one main and two outrigger floats. Several proposals had been received in response to the requirement, and orders were placed for Arado monoplane and Focke-Wulf biplane prototypes.

Initial evaluation in the summer of 1937 removed the Focke-Wulf

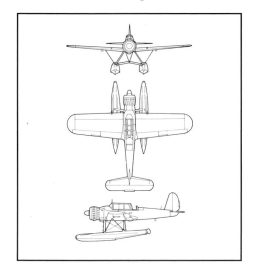

Arado Ar 196A-3

ARADO Ar 196A-3
Role: Shipborne reconnaissance floatplane
Crew/Accommodation: Two
Power Plant: One 960 hp BMW 132K air-cooled radial
Dimensions: Span 12.4 m (40.68 ft); length 11 m (36.09 ft); wing area 28.4 m² (305.6 sq ft)
Weights: Empty 2,990 kg (6,593 lb); MTOW 3,730 kg (8,225 lb)
Performance: Maximum speed 310 km/h (193 mph) at 4,000 m (13,120 ft); operational ceiling 7,000 m (22,960 ft); range 1,070 km (665 miles)
Load: Two 20 mm cannon and two 7.9 mm machine guns, plus 100 kg (210 lb) of bombs

The Arado Ar 196A floatplane

VOUGHT OS2U KINGFISHER (U.S.A.)

OS2U-2 Kingfisher

To replace its O3U Corsair biplane operated by the U.S. Navy in the scouting role, Vought produced its VS.310 design with a cantilever monoplane wing in the low/mid-position, a portly fuselage with extensive glazing, and provision for fixed landing gear that could be of the tailwheel or float type, the latter based on a single central float and two stabilizing floats under the wings.

The U.S. Navy ordered a single XOS2U-1 prototype, and this first flew in March 1938 in landplane configuration with the 336-kW (450-hp) Pratt & Whitney R-985-4 Wasp Junior radial; in May of the same year the type was first flown in floatplane form. The trial programme was completed successfully, and the type was ordered into production as the OS2U-1 with the R-985-48 engine.

Production totalled 54 aircraft, and in August 1940 these became the first catapult-launched observation/scout aircraft to serve on American capital ships. Further production embraced 158 examples of the OS2U-2 with the R-985-50 engine and modified equipment, and 1,006 examples of the OS2U-3 with the R-985-AN-2 engine, self-sealing fuel tanks, armour protection, and armament comprising two 7.7-mm (0.303-in) machine guns (one fixed and the other trainable) and two 147-kg (325-lb) depth charges. The type was also operated by inshore patrol squadrons in the anti-submarine air air-sea rescue roles, proving an invaluable asset. Some aircraft were supplied to Central and South American nations, and 100 were transferred to the Royal Navy as Kingfisher Mk I trainers and catapult-launched spotters. Nothing came of the planned OS2U-4 version with a more powerful engine and revised flying surfaces that included a straight-tapered tailplane and narrow-chord wings with full-span flaps and square cut tips.

A Vought OS2U-2 Kingfisher floatplane

VOUGHT-SIKORSKY 0S2U-3 KINGFISHER
Role: Shipborne (catapult-launched) reconnaissance
Crew/Accommodation: Two
Power Plant: One 450 hp Pratt & Whitney R-985-AN-2 or -8 air-cooled radial
Dimensions: Span 10.95 m (35.91 ft); length 10.31 m (33.83 ft); wing area 24.34 m² (262.00 sq ft)
Weights: Empty 1,870 kg (4,123 lb); MTOW 2,722 kg (6,000 lb)
Performance: Maximum speed 264 km/h (164 mph) at 1,676 m (5,500 ft); operational ceiling 3,962 m (13,000 ft); radius 1,296 km (805 miles)
Load: Two 0.3 in machine guns, plus up to 295 kg (650 lb) bombload

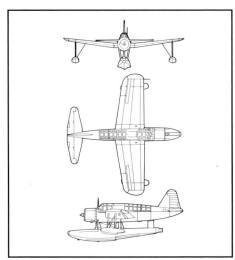

Vought OS2U Kingfisher

AVRO SHACKLETON (United Kingdom)

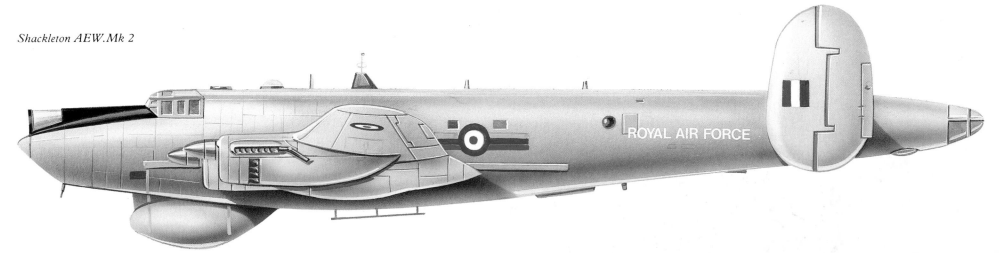

Shackleton AEW.Mk 2

To give the Lancaster a long-range capability at high altitude, Avro planned the Lancaster Mk IV, but this Type 694 emerged as so different an aeroplane that it was given the name Lincoln. The prototype flew in June 1944 and, although plans were laid for 2,254 aircraft, British post-war production amounted to only 72 Lincoln B.Mk1s and 465 Lincoln B.Mk 2s. Canada completed one

Lincoln B.Mk XV, but Australia built 43 Lincoln B.Mk 30s and 30 Lincoln B.Mk 30As, and 20 of these were later modified to Lincoln B.Mk 31 standard together with a longer nose accommodating search radar and two operators.

Meanwhile, experience with the Lancaster in the maritime role after World War II made the British decide to develop a specialized aeroplane as

the Lincoln GR.Mk III with the wing and landing gear of the bomber married to a new fuselage, revised empennage, and Rolls-Royce Griffon engines, each driving a contra-rotating propeller unit. Later renamed Shackleton, the first example of the new type flew in March 1949, leading to production of the Shackleton GR.Mk 1 (later MR.Mk 1) with two Griffon 57As and two Griffon 57s, and the Shackleton MR.Mk 1A with four Griffon 57As. The Shackleton MR.Mk 2 had revised armament and search radar with its antenna in a retractable 'dustbin' rather than a chin radome, while the definitive

Shackleton MR.Mk 3 was considerably updated, lost the dorsal turret but gained underwing hardpoints, and changed to tricycle landing gear. Eight MR.Mk3s also went to the South African air force. Twelve MR.Mk 2s were converted in the 1970s into Shackleton AEW.Mk 2 airborne early-warning aircraft for the RAF, especially equipped with specialist radar, remaining in service until the arrival of Boeing E-3s.

Avro Shackleton MR.Mk 3

AVRO SHACKLETON AEW.Mk 2
Role: Airborne early warning
Crew/Accommodation: Ten
Power Plant: Four 2,456 hp Rolls-Royce Griffon 57A water-cooled inlines
Dimensions: Span 36.52 m (119.83 ft); length 28.19 m (92.5 ft); wing area 135.45 m² (1,458 sq ft)
Weights: Empty 25,583 kg (56,400 lb); MTOW 44,452 kg (98,000 lb)
Performance: Cruise speed 322 km/h (200 mph) at 3,050 m (10,000 ft); operational ceiling 5,852 m (19,200 ft); endurance 16 hours
Load: None, other than APS 20 long-range search radar

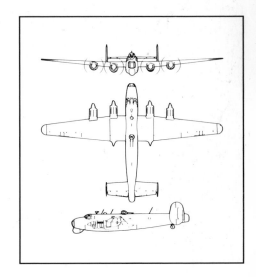

Avro Shackleton MR.Mk 1

59

LOCKHEED MARTIN P-3 ORION (U.S.A.)

P-3C Orion

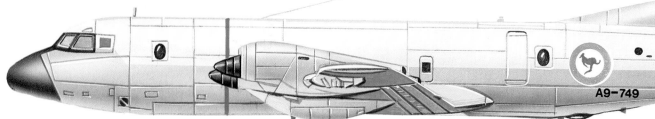

In 1957 the U.S. Navy required a maritime patrol type to supplant the piston-engined Lockheed P2V Neptune, and stressed the urgency of the programme by agreeing to the development of the type on the basis of an existing civil airframe. Lockheed's Model 85 proposal was therefore based on the airframe/powerplant combination of the relatively unsuccessful Model 188 Electra turboprop-powered airliner, though with the fuselage shortened by 2.24 m (7 ft 4 in) as well as modified to include a weapons bay in the lower fuselage.

The YP3V-1 prototype first flew in November 1959, and while the initial production variant was delivered from August 1962 with the designation P3V-1, it was redesignated P-3A in 1962. By the end of U.S. Orion production in 1996, 649 had been delivered to the U.S. Navy and forces abroad while others continued to be built by Kawasaki in Japan. The original 157 P-3As were powered by 3,356-kW (4,500-shp) Allison T56-A-10W turboprops and, though the initial aircraft had the same tactical system as the P2V-7, the 109th and later aircraft had the more advanced Deltic system that was then retrofitted to the earlier machines. The 145 P-3Bs were given the same Deltic system, but were powered by 3,661-kW (4,910-shp) T56-A-14 engines and were delivered with provision for the launch of AGM-12 Bullpup air-to-surface missiles. The final version was the P-3C, which retain the airframe/powerplant combination of the P-3B but was given the A-NEW ASW avionics system with new sensors and controls. In 1975 the first of a series of Update models was introduced, aimed to increase operational effectiveness, the last being Update III, in 1984. There were also several export models including the CP-140 Aurora for Canada that combined the P-3C's airframe and powerplant with the electronics of the Lockheed S-3 Viking carrierborne anti-submarine platform; the related Canadian CP-140A Arcturus has no ASW equipment and is used for surveillance. The U.S. Navy also took in electronic surveillance models as EP-3 Aries IIs, plus various transport, trainer and the research models RP-3, while an airborne early warning version P-3AEW went to U.S. Customs.

Lockheed Martin P-3C in Australian service as the AP-3C

LOCKHEED ORION P-3C Update III ORION
Role: Long-range maritime patrol and anti-submarine
Crew/Accommodation: Ten
Power Plant: Four 4,910-shp Allison T56-A-14 turboprops
Dimensions: Span 30.38 m (99.66 ft); length 35.6 m (116.8 ft); wing area 120.8 m² (1,300 sq ft)
Weights: Empty 27,892 kg (61,491 lb); MTOW 64,410 kg (142,000 lb)
Performance: Maximum speed 761 km/h (466 mph) at 4,572 m (15,000 ft); operational ceiling 10,485 m (34,400 ft); radius of action 3,836 km (2,384 miles)
Load: Up to 9,072 kg (20,000 lb) of weapons and sonobuoys

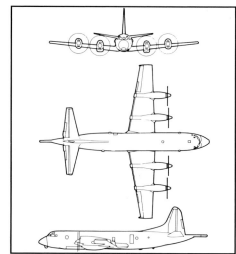

Lockheed Martin P-3C Orion

BRITISH AEROSPACE NIMROD (United Kingdom)

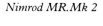

Nimrod MR.Mk 2

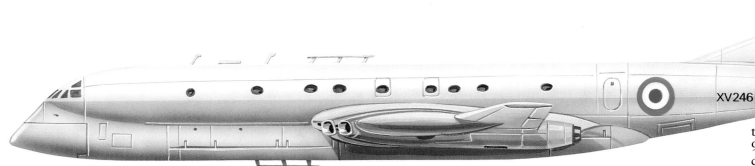

The Nimrod was developed on the aerodynamic and structural basis of the Comet 4 airliner as a jet-powered maritime patroller to replace the piston-engined Avro Shackleton. The Nimrod looks remarkably similar to the Comet 4, but features a fuselage shortened by 1.98 m (6 ft 6 in) and deepened to allow the incorporation of a weapons bay 14.78 m (48 ft 6 in) long below the wide tactical compartment, a turbofan

powerplant for much improved reliability and range (especially in the patrol regime with two engines shut down), and highly advanced mission electronics including radar, MAD and an acoustic data-processing system using dropped sonobuoys. Wings, tailplane and landing were similar to those of Comet 4C, though the landing gear was strengthened, and the first prototype flew in May 1967 as a conversion of a Comet 4C. Successful trials led to production of 46 Nimrod MR.Mk 1s with EMI ASV-21D search radar and

Emerson ASQ-10A magnetic anomaly detector in a tail 'sting'.

A variant of this baseline version became the Nimrod R.Mk 1, a special electronic intelligence variant of which three were produced. Further development in the electronic field led to the improved Nimrod MR.Mk 2, of which 35 were produced by conversion of MR.Mk 1 airframes with EMI Searchwater radar, Loral ESM in wingtip pods (to complement the original Thomson-CSF ESM system in a fintop fairing), and a thoroughly upgraded

tactical suite with a Marconi ASQ-901 acoustic data-processing and display system allowing use of many active and passive sonobuoy types. Redelivery of Mk 2s began in 1979, the addition of inflight refuelling later adding a 'P' to the designation.

Under current development is the Nimrod 2000 or MRA.Mk 4, initially for the RAF from 2003 and 21 are being produced by major rework of existing aircraft, having new mission systems, a 2-man cockpit with modern LCD screen displays, new wings and other components, BMW Rolls-Royce BR710 turbofans, Searchwater 2000 radar, other advanced avionics and more.

Nimrod MR.Mk 1

BRITISH AEROSPACE NIMROD MR.Mk 2P
Role: Long-range maritime reconnaissance/anti-submarine
Crew/Accommodation: Twelve
Power Plant: Four 5,440-kgp (11,995-lb s.t.) Rolls-Royce Spey Mk 250 turbofans
Dimensions: Span 35 m (114.83 ft); length 39.32 m (129 ft); wing area 197 m² (2,121 sq ft)
Weights: Empty 39,000 kg (86.000 lb); MTOW 87,090 kg (192,000 lb)
Performance: Maximum speed 926 km/h (576 mph) at 610 m (2,000 ft); operational ceiling 12,802 m (42,000 ft); endurance 12 hours
Load: Up to 6,120 kg (13,500 lb) including up to nine Stingray lightweight anti-submarine torpedoes, Harpoon missiles, depth charges, mines and/or cluster bombs

Nimrod MR.Mk 1

INDEX